# GCSE ENGLISH

## for OCR

**Gravesend Learning Technology Centre**
Tel: (01322) 629615
E-mail: LTC_Gravesend@nwkcollege.ac.uk
**Four Weekly Loan**
This item has been issued for four weeks.
Fines will be charged for late returns

Chris Barcock
Chief Examiner

Liz Hanton

Mel Peeling

Alison Ross

Christine Shaw Smith

OCR
RECOGNISING ACHIEVEMENT

OXFORD
UNIVERSITY PRESS

Official Publisher Partnership

# Contents

# Unit 3: Information and Ideas

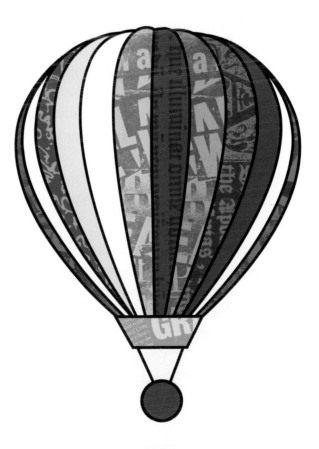

# How to Use This Book

## Welcome to your GCSE English Language course!

The aim of this book is to prepare you for the OCR GCSE English Language examinations and Controlled Assessments. It has been written in consultation with OCR by a chief examiner and several practising teachers and Teachit contributors. This means that you will not only find plenty of fun and engaging activities to build your skills and knowledge, but also all the help and advice you need to tackle your assessments.

This book includes a range of useful **features**.

- **How to approach** sections outline the requirements of each part of the specification.
- **Preparing for** sections offer invaluable guidance on preparing for exams and Controlled Assessments to help you achieve your best results.
- **Learning checklists** at the start of each chapter help to explain the Assessment Objectives and tell you what skills will be covered in the pages that follow.
- **Functional Skills** boxes provide real-life application of your GCSE knowledge, helping to prepare you for the stand-alone Functional Skills assessments.
- **Examiner's tips** boxes contain useful advice from a real examiner.
- **Exam-style questions** and sample Controlled Assessment tasks modelled on real papers help you to practise and feel more confident.
- **Sample student responses** show examples of high- and low-scoring answers with detailed Examiner's comments to help you develop and improve your own work.
- **Try This!** pages give you a chance to take a break from the specification requirements and get to grips with English Language in a fun and creative way.

The book is organized according to the OCR GCSE English Language specification, which is made up of **three units**:

- Unit 1: Extended Literary Text and Imaginative Writing
- Unit 2: Speaking, Listening and Spoken Language
- Unit 3: Information and Ideas

Each of these units is assessed using different Assessment Objectives, and the chapters in this book help you to learn what is expected from you for each objective. The four **Assessment Objectives** (AOs) for English Language are:

### AO1 Speaking and listening

- Speak to communicate clearly and purposefully; structure and sustain talk, adapting it to different situations and audiences; use Standard English and a variety of techniques as appropriate.
- Listen and respond to speakers' ideas and perspectives, and how they construct and express meanings.
- Interact with others, shaping meanings through suggestions, comments and questions and drawing ideas together.
- Create and sustain different roles.

### AO2 Study of spoken language

- Understand variations in spoken language, explaining why language changes in relation to contexts.
- Evaluate the impact of spoken language choices in their own and others' use.

### AO3 Studying written language

- Read and understand texts, selecting material appropriate to purpose, collating from different sources and making comparisons and cross references as appropriate.
- Develop and sustain interpretations of writers' ideas and perspectives.
- Explain and evaluate how writers use linguistic, grammatical, structural and presentational features to achieve effects and engage and influence the reader.

### AO4 Writing

- Write to communicate clearly, effectively and imaginatively, using and adapting forms and selecting vocabulary appropriate to task and purpose in ways that engage the reader.
- Organize information and ideas into structured and sequenced sentences, paragraphs and whole texts, using a variety of linguistic and structural features to support cohesion and overall coherence.
- Use a range of sentence structures for clarity, purpose and effect, with accurate punctuation and spelling.

# Unit I

## Extended Literary Text and Imaginative Writing

## HOW TO APPROACH UNIT I

### How will this unit be tested?

This unit tests reading and writing and accounts for 30% of the course as a whole. The unit will be tested by Controlled Assessment, which are supervised, extended writing sessions.

You will complete two tasks:
- **Section A:** a response of up to **1600 words** on an Extended Literary Text.
- **Section B:** two pieces of Imaginative Writing totalling up to **1200 words**.

You will have **four** hours to complete each of the above tasks, although this time may be split up into shorter sessions. At the end of each session your teacher will collect your work and lock it away until the next session.

Before you write your responses in the Controlled Assessment, you will spend time preparing your work in lessons.

### What will the tasks be?

For **Section A** you will answer **one** question on **one** literary text. The text may be prose, drama, poetry or literary non-fiction. It may be one of a range of texts set by the exam board or a text chosen by your teacher.

In **Section B** you have a choice of tasks. You can **either** produce:
- a piece of personal and imaginative writing, **or**
- a piece of prose fiction.

Whichever task you choose in Section B, you will need to produce **two pieces of writing**. Both pieces of writing will be linked in some ways but will also allow you to show that you can write in a variety of forms.

## How will my work be marked?

Your writing in this section will be marked against Assessment Objective 3, which tests the skills listed below.

- **Read and understand texts, selecting material appropriate to purpose, collating from different sources and making comparisons and crossreferences as appropriate.**

  You need to show that you can carefully select and analyse relevant sections of the text in order to meet the specific requirements of the task. You should have knowledge of the text as a whole but the examiner particularly wants to see how you respond to the detail of the description and dialogue, making links between related sections as part of your analysis.

- **Develop and sustain interpretations of writers' ideas and perspectives.**

  This is where you explore the writer's concerns in the text. For example, many writers are interested in conflicts between order and disorder; others in the way people attempt to persuade others to behave in a particular way. To gain marks here, you need to identify and respond to the writer's viewpoint.

- **Explain and evaluate how writers use linguistic, grammatical, structural and presentational features to achieve effects and engage and influence the reader.**

  The texts you study will challenge you and suggest alternative ways of looking at issues and ideas. This Assessment Objective requires you to look at, and comment on, the writer's choice of language and structure, and how these choices allow the writer to influence the reader.

## When will the tasks be set?

The tasks will be available over a year in advance of the final assessment, so there is plenty of time for you and your teacher to move from a general study of the text to a more specific focus relating to the task.

## LEARNING CHECKLIST

In this chapter you will learn to:

1 Understand texts, selecting parts that are relevant to certain ideas and comparing texts where necessary.
2 Interpret writers' ideas and viewpoints.
3 Explain how writers use language, style and form to create specific effects to engage readers and to influence them.

**AO3**

## Meaning, ideas and influence

This chapter will help you sharpen your skills in reading and analysing a variety of different texts, both poetry and prose. Once you understand the overall meaning, you will practise making more specific points and supporting these with quotations or examples from the text.

As well as identifying the main ideas, you will focus on how writers use different language, styles and forms to influence the reader to think in a certain way or to experience a range of emotions.

### ACTIVITY 1

How many emotions can you think of that a writer might try to provoke from a reader? Draw a spider diagram in which you name as many emotions as you can or draw facial expressions to illustrate different feelings.

## Understanding surface meaning

Before you can start to analyse any text in detail, it is essential that you take the time to understand what it is all about. This 'surface meaning' is also known as the 'literal meaning'.

Sometimes, it may not be possible to gain a complete sense of what the literal meaning is straight away. However, taking note of what you **do** know is always a good place to start.

Sorry, can't make it tmrw ☹

Hi Sam. Looking forward to the party! ☺

## ACTIVITY 2

Read the poem on the right.

**a** What is it about? Start by looking at the title. What clues does it give you about the subject of the poem or the ideas it will address?

**b** When you have read through the whole poem once, complete this sentence:

*On the surface, 'About His Person' is about...*

Remember to support your point by choosing an appropriate quotation from the text.

### 'About His Person'
### by Simon Armitage

Five pounds fifty in change, exactly,
a library card on its date of expiry.

A postcard, stamped,
unwritten, but franked,

a pocket-size diary slashed with a pencil
from March twenty-fourth to the first of April.

A brace of keys for a mortise lock,
an analogue watch, self-winding, stopped.

A final demand
in his own hand,

a rolled-up note of explanation
planted there like a spray carnation

but beheaded, in his fist.
A shopping list.

A giveaway photograph stashed in his wallet,
a keepsake banked in the heart of a locket.

No gold or silver,
but crowning one finger

a ring of white unweathered skin.
That was everything.

So far you have identified the literal meaning of the text – that's only the first step. Turn over to find out how to gain a much higher grade by reading beneath the surface to discover the **implied meaning**.

## Understanding implied meaning

To gain a top grade, you need to show that you can read with insight. This means that you must go beyond the surface or literal meaning to the ideas beneath. This is called the **implied meaning**. Often the writer won't make the implied meaning obvious. Part of the pleasure of reading is working this out.

In the poem 'About His Person' (see page 9), much is suggested or implied about the man's life and the way he died.

### ACTIVITY 3

Imagine you are a detective. What clues can you find about:

- the man's life?
- how he died?

Use the grid below to help you. The first row has been completed for you.

| CLUES FROM THE POEM | WHAT THIS SUGGESTS ABOUT THE MAN'S LIFE | WHAT THIS SUGGESTS ABOUT HOW HE DIED |
|---|---|---|
| 'a library card on its date of expiry.' | He led a fairly ordinary life and enjoyed simple, inexpensive pleasures such as reading. | The fact the library card was about to expire could suggest that the man couldn't see the point of renewing it. Perhaps he had given up hope and may even have realized that he was about to die. |

Like a detective, you can expect there to be a number of different ways of reading or interpreting each clue. Your job is to make the best judgement based on the evidence available, that is the words in the poem.

You have explored some of the implied meanings in the poem, now take a closer look at the writer's choice of language and the effect that it has upon the reader. Writers often make readers work hard to decide what their words really mean. Words or lines that carry more than one meaning, or cases where the meaning is not clear, can be described as **ambiguous**.

## ACTIVITY 4

The last line of the poem 'About His Person' – 'That was everything' – has more than one meaning. What possible meanings might it have?

### EXTENSION TASK

You may be asked to make connections between different parts of a writer's work that feature the same theme or way of writing. Read 'Poem', also by Simon Armitage. This is about another unidentified male and his relationships with the women in his life.

**a** 'Poem' also contains some **ambiguous lines**. Identify them and explain the possible meanings.

**b** Compare the effects of ambiguity in each poem.

## 'Poem'
### by Simon Armitage

And if it snowed and snow covered the drive
he took a spade and tossed it to one side.
And always tucked his daughter up at night.
And slippered her the one time that she lied.

And every week he tipped up half his wage.
And what he didn't spend each week he saved.
And praised his wife for every meal she made.
And once, for laughing, punched her in the face.

And for his mum he hired a private nurse.
And every Sunday taxied her to church.
And he blubbed when she went from bad to worse.
And twice he lifted ten quid from her purse.

Here's how they rated him when they looked back:
sometimes he did this, sometimes he did that.

## EXAMINER'S TIPS

✔ Remember, poems are open to interpretation; they do not always have one set meaning.

✔ Be confident in expressing your own opinions, making sure that you back up what you say with evidence from the text.

## Analysing language choices

In his novel *Tsotsi*, Athol Fugard describes life in a
poverty-stricken township in South Africa, where some
young black people turn to crime and violence in order to
survive. They are the victims of apartheid, the political
system that made black people second-class citizens,
denying them the rights and opportunities enjoyed by
the whites. Tsotsi is a young gang leader.

### ACTIVITY 5

In the extract below, Tsotsi sets out with his gang
to commit a murder. How does the writer use
language to depict:

**a** the township

**b** Tsotsi and his gang?

### From *Tsotsi*
### by Athol Fugard

The street they took was crooked and buckled as bad as
the corrugated iron fences they passed on the side and
Tsotsi led them a way that was sharp with stones, and eyes, and dog's
teeth. It was dusty and the end of a day, but still light, when they left
the room […] the four men passing that moment were harbingers of
the night, that moment gone now because *they* had passed and rooms
were suddenly grey and cold and mothers calling their children off the
streets where shadows were running like rats after the four pipers.

And Tsotsi knew it. Knowing it not only as a fact as big as the brave
men who stepped aside to let him pass, and the shopkeeper who
hurried out to board up his windows and bolt his door, or as small as
fatherless children and the whispers of hate that scuttled away down
the alleys, he knew it also as his meaning. Life had taught him no other.
[…] The big men, the brave ones, stood down because of him, the fear
was of him, the hate was for him. It was all there because of him. He
knew he *was*. He knew he was there, at that moment, leading the others
to take one on the trains.

That is why in his passing down the crooked street, men looked the
other way and women wept into the dust.

Here is an extract from a student's response:

**STUDENT**

Language is used to show the poverty and corruption in the township. The street is described as 'crooked' and 'buckled' suggesting that it is deformed and leading the way to something bad. This is reinforced by the image of sharp stones and eyes, and dog's teeth, all of which seem hostile, unfriendly and dangerous. The simile of shadows 'running like rats' after the gangsters gives an image of them drawing out the evil, dangerous elements of the town, leading them towards death, like in the tale of the Pied Piper.

Note how this student has embedded **short quotations** into her sentences. This is a good style to use as it will show the examiner that you are able to be selective and choose the most relevant words to prove your point. This student also carefully explains why these particular words are effective and what impression they have on the reader.

## ACTIVITY 6

How does the language in the extract on page 12 build up a sense of suspense about what is going to happen next?

Copy and complete the grid below, and use it to help structure your answer. You may wish to include other quotations as well.

| QUOTATIONS | EFFECT ON THE READER |
|---|---|
| 'rooms were suddenly grey and cold' | |
| 'mothers calling their children off the streets' | |
| 'the whispers of hate that scuttled away down the alleys' | |
| 'men looked the other way' | |
| 'women wept into the dust' | |

## EXTENSION TASK

What does the reference to the tale of the Pied Piper suggest about the outcome of events? If you are not familiar with this tale, look it up.

## The effect of language patterns

In *Of Mice and Men*, John Steinbeck uses language for a variety of different effects: from creating believable dialogue to condemning the injustice that was present in 1930s America. Here, you will identify how Steinbeck uses both individual images and **patterns of language** to create a vivid setting and to bring his characters to life.

### From *Of Mice and Men*
### by John Steinbeck

[…] On the sandy bank under the trees the leaves lie deep and so crisp that a lizard makes a great skittering if he runs among them. Rabbits come out of the brush to sit on the sand in the evening, and the damp flats are covered with the night tracks of 'coons, and with the spread pads of dogs from the ranches, and with the split-wedge tracks of deer that come to drink in the dark. […]

Evening of a hot day started the little wind to moving among the leaves. The shade climbed up the hills toward the top. On the sand banks the rabbits sat as quietly as little gray, sculptured stones. And then from the direction of the state highway came the sound of footsteps on crisp sycamore leaves. The rabbits hurried noiselessly for cover. A stilted heron labored up into the air and pounded down river.

## ACTIVITY 7

a  Read the description of the clearing above and then complete the grid on the right.

b  Which of the animals listed are described as making a sound in the extract?

c  What is the significance of the way the lizards and men break the silence of this otherwise peaceful and idyllic scene?

| ANIMALS IN THE EXTRACT | DO THE ANIMALS APPEAR LATER IN THE NOVEL? AND IF SO, HOW? | WHAT DO THE ANIMALS REPRESENT? |
|---|---|---|
| Dogs | Candy's dog is shot by Carlson. | It represents survival of the fittest. Once the dog became old and unfit it was killed. Similarly, Candy was about to be sacked because he was old and had lost his hand. |

UNIT 1

Animal imagery is another language pattern that Steinbeck uses in this novel. He uses it to help create convincing characters. For example, throughout the novel Lennie is compared to a number of animals.

## ACTIVITY 8

The spider diagram features the animals that Lennie is compared to. Copy the diagram outline below.

**a** Write down a quotation in which Lennie is described as, or likened to, each animal in the diagram below (examples can be found in Chapter 1 of the novel).

**b** What does the comparison suggest about Lennie's physical appearance and personality?

### EXTENSION TASK

References to hands form a recurring pattern of imagery within the novel. For instance, Curley has his hand crushed by Lennie. Produce a spider diagram identifying hand references in the novel. For each one, include a quotation and explain what it stands for.

Overall, what do hands represent within the novel?

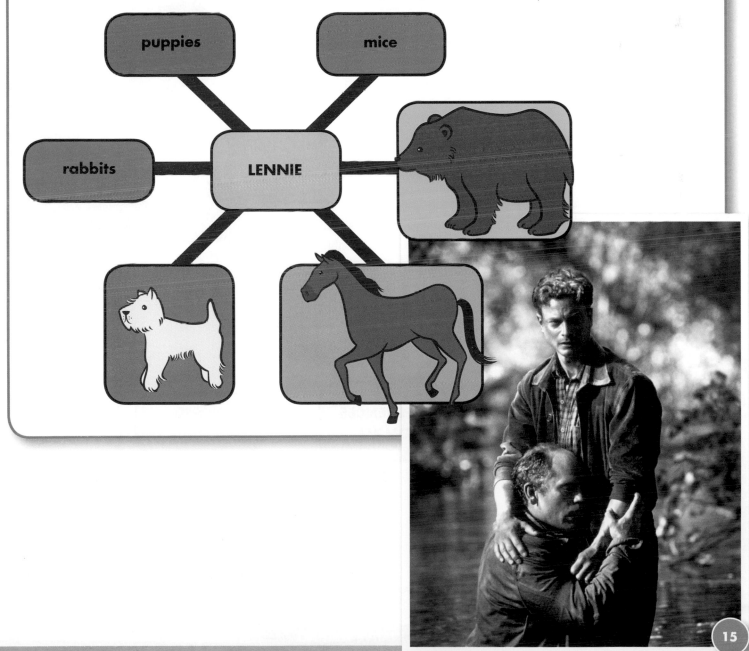

## LEARNING CHECKLIST

In this chapter you will learn to:

**1** Understand texts, selecting parts that are relevant to certain ideas and comparing texts where necessary.

**2** Interpret writers' ideas and viewpoints.

**3** Explain how writers use language, style and form to create specific effects to engage readers and to influence them.

**AO3**

## Responding to texts differently

As readers, we may interpret the same text differently according to our own backgrounds and views. Look at the image on the right. Some of you might see a beautiful young lady, while others might see an unattractive old woman. It depends on your perspective and how you look at it. It's the same with words on a page; people can read them in different ways.

### ACTIVITY 1

Which aspects of your life, background and opinions might influence how you read a text? Copy and complete the spider diagram below, identifying the factors that might affect how you feel about a text.

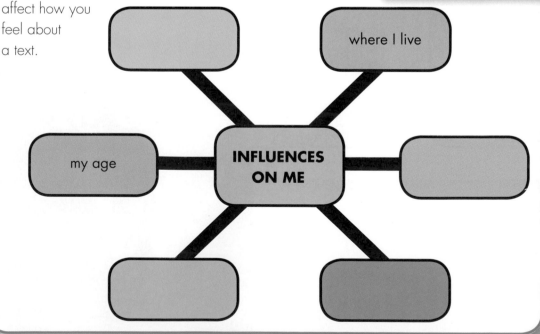

where I live

my age

**INFLUENCES ON ME**

UNIT 1

So, there is a vast range of factors that can influence **what** you read and **how** you read. These factors are all likely to affect how you interpret the words on a page.

## ACTIVITY 2

Read the view about men expressed in the opening line of *Pride and Prejudice*:
'It is a truth universally acknowledged that a single man in possession of a good fortune must be in want of a wife.'

**a** Look back at the spider diagram you produced for Activity 1. Which factors influence how you respond to the ideas within this line?

**b** How might this quotation have been viewed differently by someone reading the novel when it was originally written, about 200 years ago?

## ACTIVITY 3

Read the extract, above, from *Pride and Prejudice* where Elizabeth attempts to reject Mr Collins's proposal of marriage.

**a** Why might a reader in Jane Austen's time have found it amusing?

**b** Would a modern reader find it humorous for any different reasons?

## EXAMINER'S TIPS

If you want to produce a top-scoring response in this section, you need to analyse the writer's perspective and intentions in detail, backing up what you say with relevant quotations and comparisons.

# From *Pride and Prejudice*
## by Jane Austen

'When I do myself the honour of speaking to you next on this subject, I shall hope to receive a more favourable answer than that you have now given me; though I am far from accusing you of cruelty at present, because I know it to be the established custom of your sex to reject a man on the first application, and perhaps you have even now said as much to encourage my suit as would be consistent with the true delicacy of the female character.'

'Really, Mr Collins,' cried Elizabeth, with some warmth, 'you puzzle me exceedingly. If what I have hitherto said can appear to you in the form of encouragement, I know not how to express my refusal in such a way as may convince you of its being one.'

## Same place, different viewpoints

Some writers express an opinion; for example, about a current affairs issue, a person or a place. Just because the writer holds a particular view, this does not mean the reader will necessarily agree with it.

Morecambe is a seaside resort in the north west of England. Read Bill Bryson's description of Morecambe in his travelogue *Notes From a Small Island* in which he recounts his journey around Britain in the late 1980s.

### From *Notes From a Small Island*
### by Bill Bryson

It is hard to say when or why Morecambe's decline started. It remained popular well into the 1950s – as late as 1956 it had 1,300 hotels and guesthouses, ten times the number it has today – but its descent from greatness had begun long before. The famous Central Pier was extensively damaged by a fire in the 1930s, then gradually sank into an embarrassing wreck. By 1990 the town officials had removed it from the local map – simply pretended that the derelict heap projecting into the sea, dominating the front, wasn't there. […]

Today Morecambe's tattered front consists largely of little-used bingo halls and amusement arcades, everything-for-£1 shops, and the kind of cut-price boutiques where the clothes are so cheap and undesirable that they can be safely put outside on racks and left unattended. Many of the shops are empty, and most of the rest look temporary. […] So low had Morecambe's fortunes sunk that the previous summer the town couldn't even find someone to take on the deckchair concession. When a seaside resort can't find anyone willing to set up deckchairs, you know that business is bad.

And yet Morecambe has its charms. Its seafront promenade is handsome and well maintained and its vast bay (174 square miles, if you're taking notes) is easily one of the most beautiful in the world, with unforgettable views across to the green and blue Lakeland hills. […]

Today almost all that remains of Morecambe's golden age is the Midland Hotel, a jaunty, cheery, radiant white art deco edifice with a sweeping, streamlined frontage erected on the seafront in 1933. […] Today the hotel is gently crumbling around the edges and streaked here and there with rust stains. Most of the original interior fittings were lost during periodic and careless refurbishments over the years, and several large Eric Gill statues that once graced the entranceway and public rooms simply disappeared, but it still has an imperishable 1930s charm.

## ACTIVITY 4

Thinking of a writer's purpose can help you to decide whether to accept or question their opinions. Bryson may have had more than one purpose when writing his description of Morecambe.

**a** With a partner, discuss **why** you think Bryson wrote his book.

**b** For each purpose you can think of, find a quotation to back it up. For example:

| Purpose | Example |
|---------|---------|
| To inform | 'as late as 1956 it had 1,300 hotels and guesthouses' |

**c** From your list, which do you think is Bryson's **main** purpose? Explain your answer.

# morecambe

**Home** | **Restoration** | **Contact us**

Morecambe, with its spectacular bay, its wide-open skies and whirling seabirds, is preparing for a new tomorrow. Culture is at the heart of it and the pace is gathering. New shops, restaurants and coffee bars are quickly replacing the jaded arcades; art has been interwoven at every step and its crowning glory, The Midland, has been lovingly restored and updated.

## ACTIVITY 5

Read the description above, featured on the website for Morecambe Tourist Board.

**a** What is the **purpose** of this paragraph?

**b** How is language used to give tourists a positive view of the resort? Pick out relevant words or phrases to support your points.

**c** Which factors might account for the differences in these two descriptions of the same place?

**d** Why might the writers' viewpoints be so different?

**e** Who might agree with the tourist board's version and who might agree with Bill Bryson's version?

### EXTENSION TASK

The paragraph from Morecambe Tourist Board addresses some of the criticisms made by Bryson in his earlier description. Find examples of these links between the two texts.

## Poetry of protest

Wilfred Owen was a poet and soldier who wrote and fought during the First World War. He was killed in action one week before the war ended in November 1918. At the start of the war, in 1914, propaganda posters such as the one featured below were common. They were produced by the government and displayed in public places, with the purpose of encouraging young men to enlist.

**ACTIVITY 6**

Look at the propaganda poster on the right.

**a** What is the message of this poster?

**b** Who is its audience? How can you tell?

**c** How do the words of the poster and presentational techniques persuade men to enlist?

**d** How might such messages have been received in 1914, when they were first communicated?

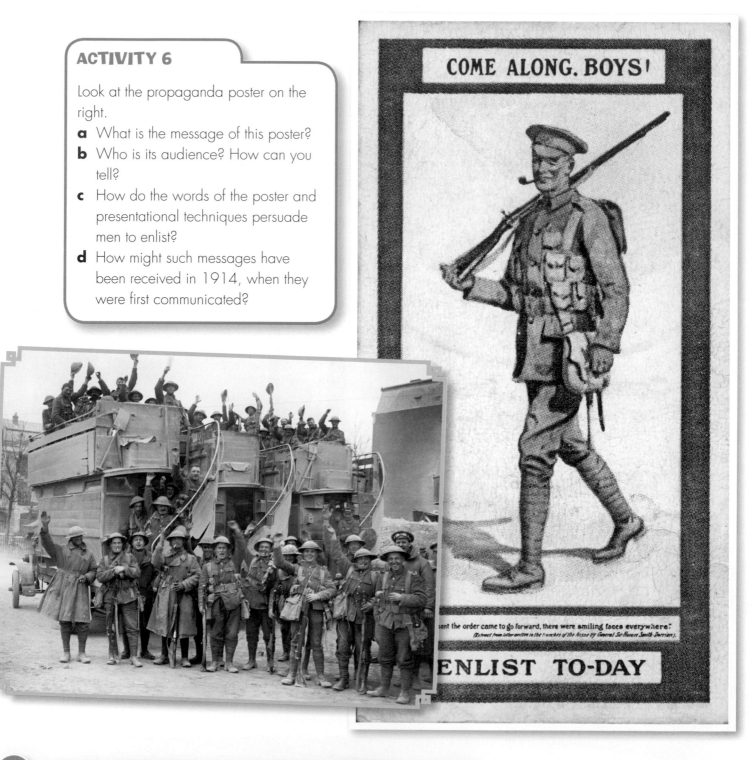

## From 'Dulce et Decorum Est'
### by Wilfred Owen

Bent double, like old beggars under sacks,
Knock-kneed, coughing like hags, we cursed through sludge,
Till on the haunting flares we turned our backs
And towards our distant rest began to trudge.
Men marched asleep. Many had lost their boots
But limped on, blood-shod. All went lame; all blind;
Drunk with fatigue; deaf even to the hoots
Of tired, outstripped Five-Nines that dropped behind.

After the first stanza, Owen goes on to describe the horrific death of a comrade in a gas attack, before challenging the reader in the final four lines of the poem:

My friend, you would not tell with such high zest
To children ardent for some desperate glory,
The old Lie: Dulce et decorum est
Pro patria mori*.

* Translates from Latin as 'It is sweet and fitting to die for one's country'.

### ACTIVITY 7

Read the first stanza (on the left) from 'Dulce et Decorum Est', Wilfred Owen's first-hand account of war, written in 1917.

**a** How is the view of war presented here different from that portrayed by the propaganda poster on page 20?

**b** Choose two images in the poem and explain how they contradict the perspective given in the propaganda poster.

### ACTIVITY 8

**a** What do the final lines of the poem mean? What point is Owen making about the messages communicated by propaganda, such as the poster on page 20?

**b** At the time when it was written, how and why might the views expressed in Owen's poem have:
- shocked and dismayed some readers
- been praised by others?

**c** Why do you think Wilfred Owen wrote this poem?

### EXTENSION TASK

As a modern reader, which view of war do you most support? Discuss your view in a group, making sure you respond to others' opinions as well as offering your own.

# Considering alternative interpretations

Thomas Hardy's 'Tony Kytes, The Arch-Deceiver', first published in the 1890s, tells the story of the hapless Tony Kytes, who finds himself in a farcical situation when he can't make up his mind which of three women to marry: Milly, Unity or Hannah. This is despite the fact that he is already engaged to Milly.

## ACTIVITY 9

From a modern perspective, the women in this story could be regarded as shallow figures of fun. Their portrayal could even be seen as insulting and patronizing. Match each view of women to the quotation that appears to support it.

| VIEW OF WOMEN | QUOTATION |
|---|---|
| Women's worth was determined purely by their physical beauty. | 'Throw over Milly? – all to marry me! How delightful!' broke out Hannah, quite loud, clapping her hands. |
| Flirtatious and competitive, women were prepared to betray each other to secure an eligible bachelor. | 'My daughter is not willing sir!' says Mr Jolliver [Hannah's father], hot and strong. |
| Women were at the mercy of their fathers' wishes. | 'If you like, Tony. You didn't really mean what you said to them?' |
| Women were compliant and weak, with Milly agreeing to marry Tony even though he has just proposed to two other women in front of her. | 'And – can you say I'm not pretty, Tony? Now look at me!' |

However, while this is one way of viewing Hardy's portrayal of women, there are other ways. It could be that it is the **treatment** of women that Hardy is being critical of, rather than the women **themselves**. Alternatively, it could be that he is using these exaggerated female caricatures to make the behaviour of men, such as Tony, seem even more comical and ridiculous.

Read the extract below from 'Tony Kytes, The Arch-Deceiver' in which Tony explains his predicament to his father.

## From 'Tony Kytes, The Arch-Deceiver'
### by Thomas Hardy

'I only asked her – that is, she asked me, to ride home.'

'She? Why, now, if it had been Milly, 'twould have been quite proper; but you and Hannah Jolliver going about by yourselves –'

'Milly's there too, father.'

'Milly? Where?'

'Under the corn-sacks! Yes, the truth is, father, I've got rather into a nunny-watch, I'm afeard! Unity Sallet is there too – yes, at the other end, under the tarpaulin. All three are in that wagon, and what to do with 'em I know no more than the dead! The best plan is, as I'm thinking, to speak out loud and plain to one of 'em before the rest, and that will settle it; not but what 'twill cause 'em to kick up a bit of a miff, for certain. Now, which would you marry, father, if you was in my place?'

## ACTIVITY 10

How might this extract suggest that Hardy is mocking Tony, rather than the three women? Look carefully at what Tony says, how he says it and what this reveals about him.

Complete each section of the student response to this question on the right. Use quotations to back up each point.

Remember that there is often more than one way of reading or interpreting a writer's ideas or viewpoints. Taking into account alternative interpretations, using tentative language such as 'might', 'alternatively' and 'could suggest' will help you to gain higher marks.

**STUDENT**

In 'Tony Kytes, The Arch-Deceiver', the three women could be interpreted as the main figures of fun in the story. They are portrayed as shallow, vain and fickle, willing to betray each other to win a proposal from Tony. One of them even says [...]

Alternatively, Tony himself could be interpreted as the main figure of fun in the story. He is portrayed as foolish and indecisive. He even has to ask his father's advice as to [...] It seems that Tony cannot control events and he gets himself into absurd situations. His description of the situation in the wagon is comical and ridiculous. He explains to his father that he ended up with [...]

Tony is portrayed as socially inept. He has no idea how to treat the women and admits that he doesn't know how to treat them any more than he would know how to treat [...] Overall, the reader could interpret Hardy's portrayal of Tony as a figure of fun, using him to mock [...]

## LEARNING CHECKLIST

**AO3**

In this chapter you will learn to:

1 Understand texts, selecting parts that are relevant to certain ideas and comparing texts where necessary.

2 Interpret writers' ideas and viewpoints.

3 Explain how writers use language, style and form to create specific effects to engage and to influence the reader.

## Language choice and audience

It is essential that writers choose language that is appropriate to their **audience** or reader. Think of it a bit like choosing the right outfit for the right occasion. For instance, you wouldn't expect your Head Teacher to turn up to school dressed like this!

### ACTIVITY 1

**a** Match the texts A–D below to the most appropriate target audience for each (i–iv).

**b** Explain your choices to a partner.

**c** Which is the least formal piece of writing? What are its features?

**d** What is the most formal piece of writing? How does the language differ here?

**A** Once upon a time there was a pink bunny called Bouncy Bob-Tail.

**B** The earth's atmosphere consists of a number of different gases, including nitrogen and oxygen.

**C** lol, wot u up 2 later will be a bangin party at mine c u there!!!

**D** Dear Madam, I am writing to you to express my concern about the amount of litter on our streets. The problem is becoming unbearable.

UNIT 1

## Language choice and purpose

A writer's **purpose** or the reason he or she is writing, also helps to determine the language he or she use.

Read the extract below from *Notes from a Small Island* by Bill Bryson, in which he describes his visit to the Stonehenge Gallery in the Salisbury Museum.

### From *Notes From a Small Island*
### by Bill Bryson

I was particularly interested in the Stonehenge Gallery because I was going there on the morrow, so I read all the instructive labels attentively. I know this goes without saying, but it really was the most incredible accomplishment. It took 500 men just to pull each sarsen [large stone], plus 100 more to dash around positioning the rollers. Just think about it for a minute. Can you imagine trying to talk 600 people into helping you drag a 50-ton stone 18 miles across the countryside, muscle it into an upright position and then saying, 'Right, lads! Another twenty like that, plus some lintels and maybe a couple of dozen nice bluestones from Wales, and we can party!' Whoever was the person behind Stonehenge was one dickens of a motivator, I'll tell you that.

## ACTIVITY 2

**a** Copy the grid below and decide what each quotation reveals about Bryson's purpose. Is it to inform, entertain or persuade or a combination?

| BRYSON'S PURPOSE | QUOTATION | FEATURES OF THE LANGUAGE USED FOR THIS PURPOSE |
|---|---|---|
| | 'It took 500 men just to pull each sarsen, plus 100 more to dash around positioning the rollers.' | Use of facts and figures; use of statements to create a factual and authoritative tone. |
| | 'Right lads! Another twenty like that... and we can party!' | |
| | 'Can you imagine trying to talk 600 people into helping you drag a 50-ton stone 18 miles...' | |

**b** Complete the final column, exploring the features of language used for each purpose.

### EXTENSION TASK

Write an entry for a travel guide about a place you know well. It should be aimed at teenagers and use some of the language features you have identified in the grid.

## Benjamin Zephaniah: language choice

Much of Benjamin Zephaniah's poetry protests against injustice: from the horrors of the slave trade to the inequality still present in British society today. Read the opening of his poem, 'Chant of a Homesick Nigga':

### From 'Chant of a Homesick Nigga'
### by Benjamin Zephaniah

There's too much time in dis dark night,
No civilians to hear me wail,
Just ghosts and rats
And there's no light
In dis infernal bloody jail.
I want my Mom
I want my twin
Or any friend that I can kiss,
I know the truth that I live in,
Still I don't want to die like dis.

If I had sword and I had shield
I would defend myself no doubt,
But I am weak
I need a meal or barrister to help me out,
I know my rights
Now tape dis talk
Of course I am downhearted,
Look sucker I can hardly walk
And the interview ain't even started.

You call me nigga, scum and wog
But I won't call you master,
The Home Secretary is not my God,
I trod earth one dread Rasta,
But in dis dumb, unfeeling cell
No decent folk can hear me cry
No God fearers or infidel
Can save me from dis Lex Loci.

### ACTIVITY 3

**a** What does it mean to you to be free?
**b** Do you think some groups of people in British society today have less freedom than others? Which ones?
**c** What should be done to ensure that everyone in Britain has equal rights?

UNIT 1

## ACTIVITY 4

**a** Where is the narrator of this poem and who is he addressing?

**b** How does the autobiographical style of this poem affect the reader?

**c** Look at Zephaniah's use of offensive, racist language in this poem – what effect does this language have on the reader?

**d** How does Zephaniah protest against injustice in this poem?

## ACTIVITY 5

**a** What is a 'chant'? When or where might someone use one?

**b** How does the style of this poem mirror that of a chant?

**c** Why might Zephaniah have decided to adopt this form?

**d** What clues are there that this poem is meant to be read aloud?

**e** Why does Zephaniah use dialect words, such as 'dis' in this poem?

### EXTENSION TASK

Compose your own protest poem. Choose an injustice that you feel strongly about. It could be a global, national or a local issue. Think carefully about the following features of your poem:

- using a strong narrative voice
- use of dialect or colloquial language
- imagery that will have impact
- rhythm and rhyme to give it pace and to make sound it effective
- repetition to emphasize key words or phrases
- the overall effect you want to create on your target audience.

### EXAMINER'S TIPS    OCR RECOGNISING ACHIEVEMENT

✓ Remember that there are often no fixed answers when it comes to poetry. People may interpret the same lines differently and both make valid observations. The key is to back up everything you say with close reference to the text.

✓ Really strong answers will take into account the fact that there are many possible points of view when interpreting poetry. You can suggest this in your answer by using language such as 'perhaps', 'implies', 'suggests' and 'I think'.

# The M25 Three

The title of Zephaniah's poem 'Three Black Males' refers to Raphael Rowe, Michael Davis and Randolph Johnson. Dubbed the 'M25 Three', they were imprisoned in 1990 for their part in a brutal murder and a series of robberies. They always claimed to be innocent but were convicted, even though some of the victims stated in court that at least one, possibly two, of the robbers was white. In 2000 their convictions were overturned and the men were released.

## 'Three Black Males'
### by Benjamin Zephaniah

Three black males get arrested
When they said they seek two whites,
Dis poet said that's expected
For we have no human rights,
We die in their police stations
We do nothing to get caught
We are only in white nations
When we win them gold in sports.

Three black males in the system
So the system just rolls on.
Can you recognise the victims
When the truth is dead and gone,
Can you recognise their anguish
When they beg you time to care
Or do you forget your language
When three black males disappear?

Raphael Rowe is not an angel
And Michael Davis ain't
Let us be straight and factual
Randolph Johnson is no saint,
The Home Office has a God complex
But that office is not great
For it does not recognise subtext
Injustice or mistakes.

Let all poets now bear witness
Let the storyteller tell
Let us deal with dis white business
Dis democracy's not well,
The cops, the judge and jury
Need some helping it does seem
And three black males with a story
Fight
So truth can reign supreme.

## ACTIVITY 6

**a** What injustices does Zephaniah protest against in this poem? List them, including a short quotation for each.

**b** Look closely at how Zephaniah's use of pronouns in the poem helps to make the poet's thoughts and feelings clear.
- To whom does the pronoun 'we' refer in the poem?
- What does this suggest about the audience for this poem?
- What does it reveal about the poet's thoughts and feelings?

**c** To whom is Zephaniah referring when he uses direct address or the pronoun 'you'? What is the effect of this?

**The Daily News**

MONDAY JULY 17 2000    www.the-daily-news.co.uk    DAILY NEWSPAPER OF THE YEAR    50p

**NEW** Money Issues Section inside

# M25 THREE FREED BY APPEAL COURT

### Freedom granted for innocent London trio after legal revoke

THE M25 THREE were dramatically freed yesterday at the Old Bailey. It occured that a leaked police report from 1999 found typed notes from Patrick Baker's police interviews, which had been heavily edited.

## EXAMINER'S TIPS

OCR
RECOGNISING ACHIEVEMENT

There are different ways to approach comparing and contrasting, such as comparing two poems line by line; analysing one first and then using the other to make comparisons; or writing about each individually and bringing them together in the conclusion. You should choose the method that that you feel most comfortable with.

## ACTIVITY 7

**a** Zephaniah uses the dialectical word 'dis' several times in the poem. Why do you think he does this?

**b** What is the effect of the repetition of 'Let' at the start of the first three lines in the final stanza?

**c** How else does Zephaniah express his anger at the treatment of the 'Three Black Males'?

### EXTENSION TASK

Compare the language of Zephaniah's protest poems about injustice within British institutions with Owen's condemnation of the soldiers' deaths in 'Anthem for Doomed Youth'.

Consider similarities and differences in their use of:
- formal/informal vocabulary and phrasing
- imagery that is shocking or poignant
- repetition of words or phrases to give emphasis and pace
- sound effects to influence the tone and mood of the poems
- rhetorical questions.

'you'  'they'

'we'

'you'  'we'

'you'  'they'  'we'

'you'  'we'  'they'

'they'  'we'

## Consolidating your reading skills

Activity 8, below, draws together the reading skills that you have practised in this chapter by setting you an essay about a poem. Before you start, read the question and the poem carefully. Use the advice given in the panels on the next page to help you plan and write your response.

### ACTIVITY 8

Look at the poem on the right. How is the criminal presented in this poem? Explain your response using evidence from the text.

Consider:

- the linguistic and grammatical features
- the structure of the poem.

### EXTENSION TASK

Compare the presentation of the criminal narrators in 'Stealing' by Carol Ann Duffy, 'Hitcher' by Simon Armitage and 'My Last Duchess' by Robert Browning. Consider how the following is conveyed:

- the mood of the narrators
- their approximate age and situation
- their personality.

Compare in particular:

- the levels of sympathy generated in the reader
- the style of language used by each narrator, for example, formal, colloquial, elaborate, direct
- the effect of any direct address to the reader.

## 'Stealing'
### by Carol-Ann Duffy

The most unusual thing I ever stole? A snowman.
Midnight. He looked magnificent; a tall, white mute
beneath the winter moon. I wanted him, a mate
with a mind as cold as the slice of ice
within my own brain. I started with the head.

Better off dead than giving in, not taking
what you want. He weighed a ton; his torso,
frozen stiff, hugged to my chest, a fierce chill
piercing my gut. Part of the thrill was knowing
that children would cry in the morning. Life's tough.

Sometimes I steal things I don't need. I joy-ride cars
to nowhere, break into houses just to have a look.
I'm a mucky ghost, leave a mess, maybe pinch a camera.
I watch my gloved hand twisting the doorknob.
A stranger's bedroom. Mirrors. I sigh like this – Aah.

It took some time. Reassembled in the yard,
he didn't look the same. I took a run
and booted him. Again. Again. My breath ripped out
in rags. It seems daft now. Then I was standing
alone among lumps of snow, sick of the world.

Boredom. Mostly I'm so bored I could eat myself.
One time, I stole a guitar and thought I might
learn to play. I nicked a bust of Shakespeare once,
flogged it, but the snowman was the strangest.
You don't understand a word I'm saying, do you?

Facts about the poem's context that may be relevant to your response:
- the poem is said to have been inspired by a real life event.
- it was published during the 1980s, a decade when unemployment in the UK peaked at three million.

Think about the methods that the poet uses to communicate her ideas. Clue: How does Duffy create a sense of natural speech? Look at the use of enjambment (when the sense of one line runs over into the next line) and colloquial language.

Read the entire poem through several times first. Start with its title and make sure that you understand its surface or literal meaning.

Consider how different readers might view the poem in different ways. Clue: Is the narrator an entirely evil character? What reasons are there to feel sorry for him or her?

Use tentative language to write about these alternative interpretations such as 'this might suggest' or 'this could show that'.

Consider the poetic structure of the dramatic monologue through which Duffy gives the criminal a voice. Clue: Why might the poem start and end with a question?

Look for patterns of language that might give you a clue to the poem's more subtle or implied meanings. Clue: In this case, look for words which have violent connotations (words which suggest violence).

Use short references or quotations from the text to support your points. You don't need to copy out entire lines – it's far more effective if you include a few relevant words from the poem within your sentence.

# PREPARING FOR UNIT 1

## SECTION A: EXTENDED LITERARY TEXT

### What do I need to learn before the assessment?

Your preparation for Section A will be guided by your teacher. By the end of your preparation you should have plenty to say about the characters, themes and the setting. You should also be confident in discussing how the writer has used language and form to express his or her ideas most effectively. You will also need to be aware of what factors may have influenced the writer, what his or her viewpoints were, and how these might be re-interpreted by readers.

### Can I take notes into the assessment?

Yes, you can take notes into the assessment. When you have completed your study of the text you should take time to produce some organized and focused notes that will help you during the assessment. These notes should form the skeleton of what you intend to write so it is vital that they link closely to the task and the Assessment Objectives.

### EXAMINER'S TIPS

- ✔ Remember that there is no right answer, so long as what you write is relevant to the task. The more original thinking you can develop the better.

- ✔ While giving a personal response is always good you **must** support what you say with reference to the language and structure the writer has chosen.

- ✔ Try to keep your notes as concise and accessible as possible so that you will be able to refer to them easily in the exam. Limit your notes to around one **A4 sheet** in length.

## What are controlled conditions?

Your assessment will take place under **controlled conditions**, which means:

- You cannot communicate with anyone during the assessment.
- You may refer to an **unannotated** copy of the text you are studying and the notes that you prepared beforehand but no other resources are permitted.
- If you are producing your response on computer all tools such as spell check and access to the Internet must be disabled.
- The work must be completed individually without help from teachers or other students.
- If the assessment is divided up into separate sessions, your work will be taken away from you at the end of each session and locked up. You will not have access to it again until the next session.

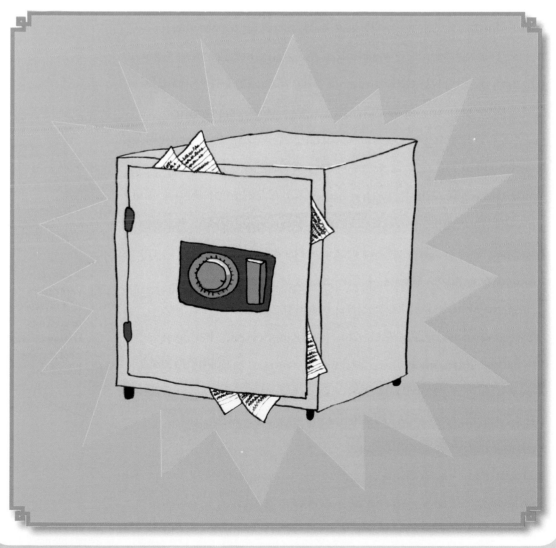

# SAMPLE TASKS

## Sample task I.I

**6** *The Withered Arm and other Wessex Tales* by Thomas Hardy

How does Thomas Hardy develop challenging female characters in any two stories from 'The Wessex Tales'?

## Student response I.I

*apt quotations and analysis of language used*

     Rhoda Brook in The Withered Arm and Lizzie Newberry in The Distracted Preacher are challenging characters. Their names suggest their roles; Rhoda means rose, a symbol of romantic love, of the sort she once shared with Lodge. Brook implies fertility, referring to their son, unlike Gertrude who 'had brought him no child'. Lizzie is described as 'a fine and extremely well made young woman... with a beautiful forehead and eyes that warmed him'. This is implied in the name 'new-berry': fresh and fruitful. This is interesting because Newberry is Lizzie's married name; her maiden name of Simpkins is less suggestive.

     Rhoda challenges her society because she survives: 'her monotonous milking at the dairy was resumed... her once abundant dark hair white and worn away...' She has faced a world dominated by men, their property and strict conventions; she survives, to continue independently, as a milkmaid, emphasizing her vital nature.

     Lizzie is challenging in the same and in different ways. She challenges the conventions of marriage, refusing to give up

*a good reference to Hardy's attitudes towards the society he lived in*

**Student response 1.1 continued**

smuggling when Stockdale asks her to marry him. Hardy develops a balanced account of the issues. 'What is money compared with a clear conscience?' Stockdale asks her and she replies, 'My conscience is clear. I know my mother, but the king I have never seen... it is a great deal to me that mother and I should live.' This is a very challenging perspective, especially as Hardy's readers were middle or upper class and would not have had much sympathy with the rural poor of Wessex.

*another good point about Hardy's perspective*

When Gertrude is introduced in the next section we can see that Hardy has created an opposite character; she appears attractive but there is more than this: 'Her face, too, was fresh in colour... soft and evanescent, like the light under a heap of rose petals.' This is telling, when we remember the inner meaning of Rhoda's name. Rhoda and Gertrude are opposites: tall/short, dark/fair and so on. The tragedy of the execution re-unites Lodge and Rhoda and spells Gertrude's end. For once Rhoda asserts herself: 'This is the meaning of Satan showed me... You are like her at last!' Gertrude's 'delicate vitality... collapsed... her blood had been 'turned' indeed - too far.' Hardy brings her story to a powerfully ironic conclusion.

*effective references to Hardy's use of plot structure and language choices*

In The Distracted Preacher, I thought like Stockdale, that Mrs Newberry was Lizzie's mother 'an elderly woman'. It is a shock to learn that Lizzie is young and attractive and even more surprising when her involvement in smuggling is revealed, again by giving us Stockdale's perspective '"You are quite right, they are barrels," said she... not without a touch of irony. Stockdale looked at her... "Not smugglers' liquor?" he said.'

Hardy sustains the role reversal between the daring Lizzie (who dresses in boots and great coat without losing her femininity) and the naïve, straight-laced Stockdale. It is very

## Student response 1.1 continued

difficult not to side with her when Hardy reaches the challenging conclusion of their relationship '"You dissent from Church, and I dissent from State" she said. "And I don't see why we are not well matched."'

Hardy has presented two female characters who, arguably, surpass the men, in vigour and independence. They take life as it comes and get on with it. Hardy changed his viewpoint on the original ending of this story. By 1912 Lizzie did not marry boring Stockdale but stuck with Owlett the smuggler in the USA.

*another well-chosen example of how Hardy uses language and structure to effect*

*excellent summary, linking back to the question*

### EXAMINER'S COMMENTS OCR
RECOGNISING ACHIEVEMENT

- An excellent response that is both personal and direct.
- Use of apt quotations to back up ideas.
- This is top-band work.

## Sample task 1.2

**7** *Of Mice and Men* by John Steinbeck

John Steinbeck refers several times to the idea of 'livin off the fatta the lan'.

Show how he uses the idea to develop the relationships between Lennie, George and the farmhands throughout the course of the novel.

# HOW TO APPROACH UNIT I

## SECTION B: IMAGINATIVE WRITING

## What will the tasks be?

You will have a choice of either:

**Personal and imaginative writing:** something based on an actual experience that you have had or something that you have witnessed

**or**

**Prose fiction:** something that may be based on an experience, but more importantly will require you to use your imagination to develop this into a new story.

Whichever option you choose, the task will consist of **two** parts: part '**a**', which is referred to as the core task, and part '**b**', which will consist of a choice of one of three linked tasks. Both part 'a' and part 'b' are worth a total of **30 marks** combined.

## How should I respond to the tasks?

It is important that your response to the core task includes a narrative line or a succession of events, although these events do not have to be presented in a linear order. Lots of good stories, for example, start near the end of the narrative and back-track to describe what happened before.

Your writing should also show some personal reflection on the circumstances you describe and a clear sense of place, time and person. It is equally important that you maintain a consistent sense of audience when you are writing.

## How will the tasks be marked?

You will be marked according to Assessment Objective 4, which covers the skills listed below.

- Write to communicate clearly, effectively and imaginatively, using and adapting forms and selecting vocabulary appropriate to task and purpose in ways that engage the reader.
- Organize information and ideas into structured and sequenced sentences, paragraphs and whole texts, using a variety of linguistic and structural features to support cohesion and overall coherence.
- Use a range of sentence structures for clarity, purpose and effect, with accurate punctuation and spelling.

# Personal and Imaginative Writing

**LEARNING CHECKLIST**

In this chapter you will learn to:

**1** Write clearly, with imagination, using suitable form and words to engage the reader.

**2** Write with a clear structure and sequence in sentences and paragraphs, using a variety of language features and techniques.

**3** Use a variety of sentence structures to create different effects, with correct punctuation and spelling.

**AO4**

## Writing to engage the reader

Personal and imaginative writing is all around us. It is in the emails we exchange with friends; in blogs and diaries; in comments we read in newspapers; in travel accounts in glossy books. With so much surrounding us, a writer has to work hard to grab and then hold the attention of the reader, particularly when writing for a wide audience.

Read the following extract from *Stephen Fry in America* where he writes about his experiences of swimming with dolphins in Florida. Think carefully about the techniques he uses to engage his readers.

---

clear explanation of events

details of people and places provide a sense of personal experience

### From *Stephen Fry in America*
### by Stephen Fry

Although the sheer pleasure of sharing the water with these amiable mammals is reason enough to do it, there has over recent years grown up the practice of Dolphin Therapy. I am due to swim with a boy, Kyle Crouch, who lives with cerebral palsy and has been coming to swim with bottle-nosed dolphins in Key Largo since he was ten years old. A young therapist called Eli has been swimming with him and supervising the sessions and it is clear that they both believe the experience has been wholly beneficial. Kyle's mother agrees.

variety of sentence structure and length, with clear punctuation

Maybe it is the sheer exhilaration of being towed, nosed, tickled, slapped, prodded, swiped and barged by the boisterous, squeaking, clicking creatures – maybe that is therapy enough, coupled with the muscular toning resulting from active time in the seawater. I certainly feel enchanted and emerge glowing with *bien-être* and a sense of one of nature's highest privileges having been bestowed upon me.

writer's personality comes through in his description of feelings

interesting vocabulary, including lists, helps the reader feel part of the experience

---

**Fry reflects on the experience in an unusual way – the reader is challenged to think.**

I ponder man's fascination with the 'higher' mammals – great apes, whales and dolphins. When in their presence it is as if we are communing with royalty or Hollywood stars. A great grin spreads over our faces. Eye contact or attention causes our hearts to beat a little faster at the knowledge of having been noticed by such supreme beings. A shame that, given this, we can't seem to share the planet with them. There won't be many species of whale and gorilla left by 2020. Perhaps the dolphins are safe so long as they continue to play.

'Dolphins,' says Eli, 'they got this instinct where they only approach those in the water who are the most nervous. They always seem to pay attention to the most vulnerable and the most wounded, physically or emotionally. You'll see them gently prod these people into play.'

'But confident people?'

'Self-satisfied people, fit people, confident people they will leave alone.'

I do not know whether to be flattered or insulted by the dolphins' very clear attentions to me.

**direct quotation gives a sense of immediacy and helps establish character**

**humour engages the reader and reveals the author's personality**

## ACTIVITY I

Write a blog entry (about 100 words) describing **either** an encounter with an animal **or** an exciting event on holiday. Try to use some of the writing techniques shown in the source text. Swap your work with a partner and underline the following:

- varied and interesting vocabulary
- where personality comes across
- detail to help the reader imagine the scene.

## EXAMINER'S TIPS

When writing your assessment task, think carefully about the most effective vocabulary and literary devices to use to have impact on your audience. Try to be imaginative in your choices: this is a good opportunity to demonstrate your creativity.

## Comparing form and purpose

The extract from a webpage, below, deals with the same sort of experience as Stephen Fry did in his book – swimming with dolphins. However, this text is more factual. It explains an activity that is on offer and allows readers to use their imaginations to plan their own swim with dolphins.

# dolphin days

## Swim Programmes

Dolphin Days offers a variety of dolphin interaction programmes, including <u>Natural Dolphin Swims</u> and <u>Structured Dolphin Swims</u>. These programmes are designed for people interested in learning more about dolphins in a safe, natural seawater environment. In addition to swimming with dolphins, visitors will take part in an educational briefing about dolphin natural history. Our highly trained staff will tell you about dolphin anatomy, social behaviour, reproductive system, echo-location, conservation programmes and what to expect during the swim. Immediately after this, you will experience our amazing in-water programme with dolphins: something you will remember for the rest of your life!

During our <u>Natural Dolphin Swims</u>, individuals will enter the water with masks, flippers and snorkels to participate in an open swimming session with

dolphins. There is no direct contact between swimmers and dolphins during these sessions. This is a truly unique experience, which simulates swimming with dolphins in the wild.

Our <u>Structured Dolphin Swims</u> are close dolphin encounters, during which each swimmer will participate in a variety of trained behaviours (for example, belly rubs, dorsal tows and kisses) with our dolphins. These activities are mediated by an experienced dolphin trainer to ensure the best experience for dolphins and visitors.

## ACTIVITY 2

Copy and complete this grid to compare the text on pages 38–39 with the text on page 40. Although both texts deal with personal experiences of swimming with dolphins, they are written in different forms and for different purposes. Stephen Fry focuses on his own experiences while exploring the USA; the website explains the learning programmes set up to help humans and dolphins interact.

Where possible, find quotations to back up your points in the grid.

| FEATURE | STEPHEN FRY IN AMERICA | DOLPHIN DAYS |
|---|---|---|
| type of text and audience | prose travel writing aimed at the general reader | |
| purpose | | |
| organization/ structure | | hyperlinks connect to different parts of the website |
| different sentence types | | |
| specialist vocabulary | | |
| narrative voice (use of first person 'I', second person 'you' or third person 'he/she/it') | | |
| use of facts/opinions | | |
| focus on personal experience | | mention of trained staff reassures prospective clients |
| accessibility (how easy it is to understand) | | |

### EXAMINER'S TIPS

Personal and imaginative writing starts with something you have imagined or experienced (and the two are often inter-related). It might be something you have read about or which has been reported to you and has caused you to stop and think. It is the key source of material for this exercise, from which you need to effectively develop and shape your narrative.

# Style, form and vocabulary

You can improve your writing by reading widely. This will help you to become familiar with different forms of texts and written styles, and to increase your vocabulary. Take the opportunity to read everyday texts, such as newspapers, magazines, websites and advertisements.

## FUNCTIONAL SKILLS TASK

**a** Explore different types of writing by researching tourism in a particular area. You could choose your local area, or elsewhere. You might start looking:

- at leaflets from a Tourist Information Centre
- at guidebooks or personal accounts of visits in a library
- on the Internet, typing in 'tourism' and the area in a search engine
- for blogs about your chosen area.

**b** With a partner or small group, look at the range of texts you have found. For each text, decide what type of text it is and what its main purpose is; for example, to advertise, to inform, to recount or to entertain.

**c** Draw a spider diagram for each text to help you analyse its style, form and key features. Use the one below to help you.

**d** Discuss how well each text fulfils its purpose, then rank the texts in order of success. Remember, not everyone will agree on the ranking order but it is important to discuss the issues that arise.

**e** Select two texts, stick them on a large sheet of paper and annotate them, pointing out their key features and any aspects that you feel are particularly effective.

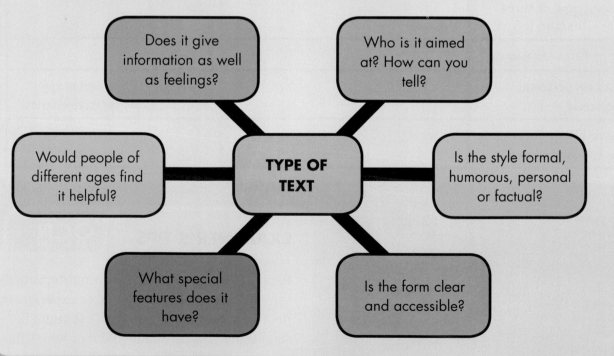

Does it give information as well as feelings?

Who is it aimed at? How can you tell?

Would people of different ages find it helpful?

**TYPE OF TEXT**

Is the style formal, humorous, personal or factual?

What special features does it have?

Is the form clear and accessible?

UNIT 1

## Widening vocabulary

One way of making your writing personal and imaginative is to choose your vocabulary carefully. This can give the reader a very clear sense of you, your attitudes, and how you feel about things. When Stephen Fry writes that he feels 'enchanted' and has 'a sense of one of nature's highest privileges having been bestowed upon me', he is showing the reader what an emotional effect swimming with dolphins had on him. 'Enchanted' makes the experience sound magical and 'privileges' implies that Fry felt both honoured and humbled.

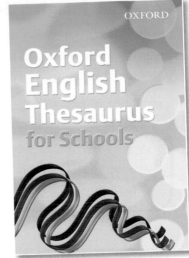

Words can build up a balanced picture of an experience. For example, Stephen Fry describes being 'towed, nosed, tickled, slapped, prodded, swiped and barged' by the dolphins. He gives us a picture of playful, slightly mischievous creatures. However, what effect would be created if the first three verbs were missed out? The overall tone would change and the dolphins would appear to be aggressive.

One of the best ways to provide variety in your writing is to use a thesaurus (the name comes from the ancient Greek for *treasure*), which lists synonyms and gives you the opportunity to try something different. If you are not familiar with one of the words listed in the thesaurus, check it out in a dictionary before you use it!

**EXAMINER'S TIPS**

Expand your vocabulary by researching and learning new words. You will be rewarded for using originality, high order vocabulary and flair appropriately in your writing.

### ACTIVITY 3

In small groups, select sentences or phrases from the material you collected about tourism and write each one in the middle of a piece of paper.

Using a thesaurus, add adjectives, adverbs or verbs to change the meaning or the tone in a variety of ways. For example, *the busy centre of Birmingham* could be the *bustling and lively centre of Birmingham*.

Discuss the effects you create and share some of the best with the rest of the class.

> beautiful, rolling
> v
> The hills of Derbyshire

# Let your imagination go to work!

On the next two pages are some extended tasks which will help you to practise your personal and imaginative writing skills. Before you start your writing, though, remember to plan your work. Use the flow diagram below to remind you of what you need to think about.

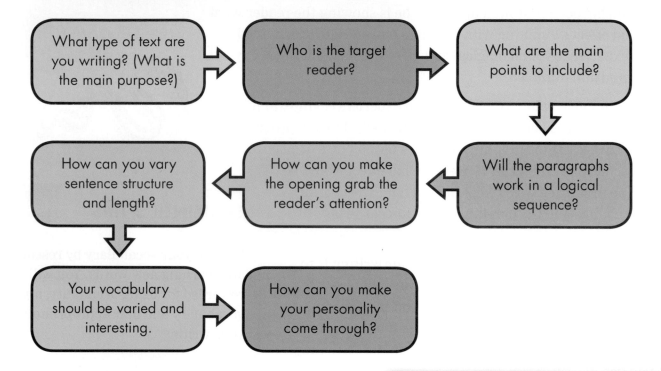

## ACTIVITY 4

**a** Write the text for a leaflet (folded A4 size) encouraging tourists to spend some time in your local area. Suggest activities and places to visit. Remember that with thought, even a dirty old canal can be 'part of our industrial heritage'! Note down what photographs you would use to accompany the text and the effects you would hope to create.

**b** Imagine you have visited the Dolphin Days aquatic park. Write a blog entry (up to 500 words) in which you describe your day.

**c** Create a webpage for an organization offering animal encounters to the general public; for example, pony trekking, dog training or sea fishing. You need to include some factual information but also use your imagination to stir the reader's interest and enthusiasm.

## EXAMINER'S TIPS

OCR
RECOGNISING ACHIEVEMENT

✔ Ensure that you make decisions about subject, genre and audience **before** you start to write.

✔ Whatever task you choose, think carefully about words, sentences and paragraphs as well as a clear overall structure.

✔ Try to be both ambitious and original in your writing.

UNIT 1

## ACTIVITY 5

Work in groups to role-play an early evening television programme which interviews people about their holiday choices and experiences. Remember you will need to have sections to introduce and link interviews with members of the public. Positive and negative experiences will help provide interest and realism.

### Holidays From Heaven and Hell

Presenter: Good evening and welcome to *Holidays From Heaven and Hell*. In this episode we will be hearing about a dream holiday in Barbados that turned into a nightmare when…

## ACTIVITY 6

Autobiographical writing is a way people can share their experiences in a public way.

Find some examples and **either**:

**a** compare the ways in which two different authors write, then try to imitate the style of one of them in an 'extra' chapter

or:

**b** imagine you have been asked to write an autobiography of your life so far. Write a chapter as it might be published in book form, or an article which might appear in your school magazine.

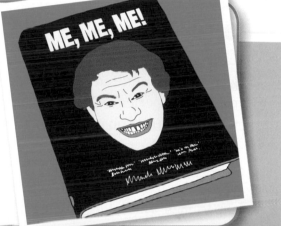

## LEARNING CHECKLIST

In this chapter you will learn to:

**AO4**

1 Write clearly, with imagination, using suitable form and words to engage the reader.

2 Write with a clear structure and sequence in sentences and paragraphs, using a variety of language features and techniques.

3 Use a variety of sentence structures to create different effects, with correct punctuation and spelling.

## Using your imagination

In Chapter 1.4, you developed skills in writing that required you to draw on personal experience. In this chapter, you will concentrate on using your imagination to create wider ranging texts which will often go far beyond your own personal experience. The spider diagram on the right shows some of the key features of this type of text.

Read through the short text which follows. Although it is brief, it contains many of the features mentioned above.

- characters to interest the reader
- detailed setting to help build atmosphere
- climax and satisfying end
- **FEATURES OF PROSE FICTION**
- set-back or crisis in story (may be several)
- dialogue
- descriptive passages

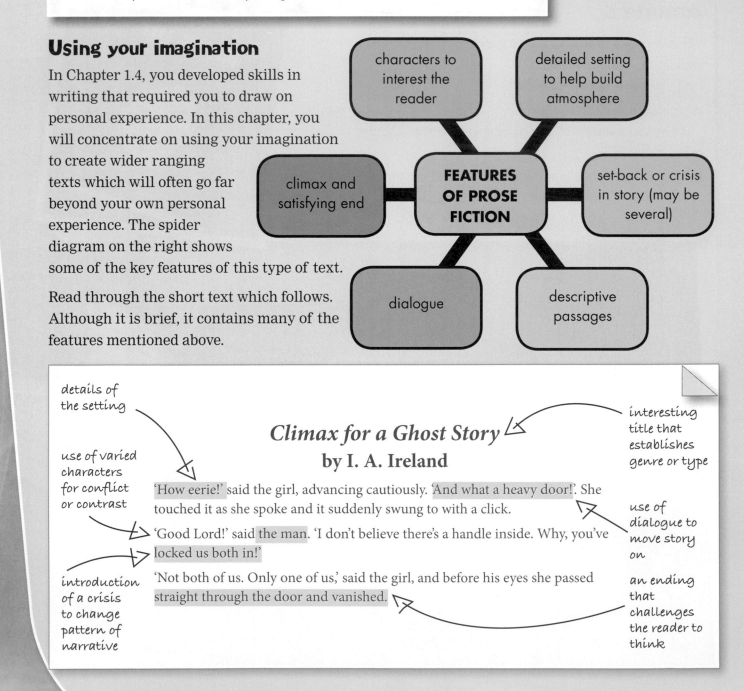

details of the setting

use of varied characters for conflict or contrast

introduction of a crisis to change pattern of narrative

### *Climax for a Ghost Story*
### by I. A. Ireland

interesting title that establishes genre or type

'How eerie!' said the girl, advancing cautiously. 'And what a heavy door!'. She touched it as she spoke and it suddenly swung to with a click.

'Good Lord!' said the man. 'I don't believe there's a handle inside. Why, you've locked us both in!'

'Not both of us. Only one of us,' said the girl, and before his eyes she passed straight through the door and vanished.

use of dialogue to move story on

an ending that challenges the reader to think

# Identifying genre

In your Controlled Assessment task for this section of Unit 1, you will be expected to complete one task that has two linked parts. You should aim to both entertain your audience and show a range of writing skills.

The most important thing is to identify the genre or type of subject, because this will influence setting, characters, dialogue and vocabulary. The examiners will be looking to see how well you can:

- get the reader interested and keep him or her wanting to read on
- organize ideas in varied sentences
- structure your writing so that it holds a reader's attention
- structure your story with paragraphs of different lengths and purposes; for example, description, action, dialogue
- use interesting and appropriate vocabulary – with correct spellings!
- punctuate accurately.

## ACTIVITY 1

This activity will help you think about planning stories by focusing on key aspects of genres, such as those in the spider diagram on page 46.

**a** Different genres are characterized by particular features. Think of character types, settings and plot elements that are relevant to the genres listed in the grid below. Some have been suggested for you. Discuss your ideas in a small group and be prepared to feed back to the rest of the class.

**b** Choose a genre that you are interested in. Use the grid to plan your own short story.

| GENRE | TYPE OF CHARACTERS | TYPE OF SETTING | PLOT ELEMENTS |
|---|---|---|---|
| Horror | mysterious characters, ghosts | | |
| Fantasy | | | magic spells, epic battles |
| Sci-fi | | futuristic or space-based settings | |
| Romance | lovers, villains | | |
| Adventure | heroic characters, villains | | |

## What makes a good opening?

The most important part of any story is the opening. If it is not sufficiently attention-grabbing, the reader is likely to give up, and no matter how strong the characters are, or how exciting the events in the rest of the story, they will be missed.

Read the three extracts which follow and think about:
- how the reader is drawn into the story
- how language is used to interest or intrigue the reader
- what you can work out about the genre of each story.

### From *The Season Ticket*
### by Jonathan Tulloch

On the southern bank of the River Tyne, where the water widens over tidal mud, stands the Metropolitan Borough of Gateshead.

Two figures, one tall, one small, were walking alongside the river. They were both teenagers. Perhaps the large one was two or three years older, but it was the smaller who led. His was a busy walk, swaying him nimbly from side to side, elbows out, setting his head in a constant swivelling, a continual searching, like a lean, trotting, urban fox. The taller one, always following at a distance of half a pace…

### From *The Curious Incident of the Dog in the Night-time*
### by Mark Haddon

It was 7 minutes after midnight. The dog was lying on the grass in the middle of the lawn in front of Mrs Shears' house. Its eyes were closed. It looked as if it was running on its side, the way dogs run when they think they are chasing a cat in a dream. But the dog was not running or asleep. The dog was dead. There was a garden fork sticking out of the dog.

## From *The Chrysalids*
## by John Wyndham

When I was quite small I would sometimes dream of a city – which was strange because it began even before I knew what a city was. But this city, clustered on the curve of a big blue bay, would come into my mind. I could see the streets, and the buildings that lined them, the waterfront, even boats in the harbour; yet, waking, I had never seen the sea, or a boat…

And the buildings were quite unlike any I knew. The traffic in the streets was strange, carts running with no horses to pull them…

## ACTIVITY 2

Compare these three openings using the points below to help you.

- Which of the three opening sentences do you like best? Why?
- Which do you think is the weakest? Why?
- Which extract gives most information about characters?

## EXTENSION TASK

Compare the openings of two or more novels, exploring ways in which the style and approach differ from these three examples.

## ACTIVITY 3

Now use what you have learnt so far to write the opening (about 100–120 words) to an adventure story called 'Lost'. Write in the centre of your page and leave space around it to highlight and annotate key features, using the guidelines (bullet points) on page 48. Remember that you need to make a strong impact in this opening section to engage the reader's interest and curiosity.

## EXAMINER'S TIPS

In this unit try to make your two pieces of writing as different in style as you can. They will be linked by theme, character or setting (or all three) so a contrast in how you write is really important.

# Developing settings

To develop a story effectively, you need more than just action and a series of events. By describing the setting, you can take your reader right into the heart of the story, helping to create atmosphere, build up tension or even help slow down a story if tension is too tight.

Use the following checklist to help you in writing descriptive passages.

- Think about the effect on your reader.
- Visualize the setting or sketch it to help you focus on key aspects.
- Use a thesaurus to help vary vocabulary.
- Use appropriate sentence structures to suit your meaning.
- Use sense impressions – sight, touch, hearing, smell, taste.

## From *The Season Ticket*
## by Jonathan Tulloch

Dejectedly they trailed into the park which had been built when Gateshead had played host to the International Garden Festival. The flower beds and walkways were gradually sinking back into the general dereliction of the area but they still retained some of the original grandeur and design. The Dunston Rocket tower block rose above them, its top floors beginning to disappear with the closing weather. It started to rain […]

The rain was growing harder. The moss which flourished on the neglected paths of the park was slippery underfoot. The trolley's wheels seemed to be squeaking louder than ever as Sewell pushed it carefully through the rank shrubberies and weed-filled flower beds.

## ACTIVITY 4

**a** Use the checklist to see how the writer of the above passage uses description. Discuss ways you could change the atmosphere by altering vocabulary. You may find it helpful to use a thesaurus.

**b** Write a description of a place you know well as it might appear on a webpage for young people moving to the area.

# Building character

To create strong believable characters in your fiction writing you need to first have a clear idea of them in your own head. Imagine how they appear, how they behave, how they think and how they respond to other characters.

All these aspects need to be linked to create credible, rounded characters that are portrayed consistently throughout your writing. Once you have a clear idea of your characters, you need to think carefully about how to convey them to your readers. Below are some suggestions.

- Use comparisons (similes and metaphors) to describe them. These can help give subtle clues about their personalities. For example, the two boys in the *Season Ticket* extract on page 48 are compared to animals. The younger boy is 'like a lean, trotting, urban fox' while his friend has 'the slow appearance of an overgrown tortoise'. What do these descriptions suggest about each boy?
- Avoid flat, detailed physical descriptions, such as 'he had brown hair'. Try to use appearance to reveal something about personality, such as 'her mop of untidy brown curls bounced up and down in time to her wild, imaginary drumming'.
- Choose the way that your characters speak with care. The way people speak usually reflects the way that they think, so make sure the two are consistent (unless a character is a deceitful villain!).

## ACTIVITY 5

Create two characters for your story 'Lost'.
- First write some notes about your characters. Use the thought bubbles around this page to help trigger ideas.
- Decide on names that suit the setting and story genre.
- Write a paragraph for each character, introducing them to your reader. Try to reveal their personalities, how other characters respond to them and give hints about their roles in the plot. Avoid flat, dull descriptions of how they look.

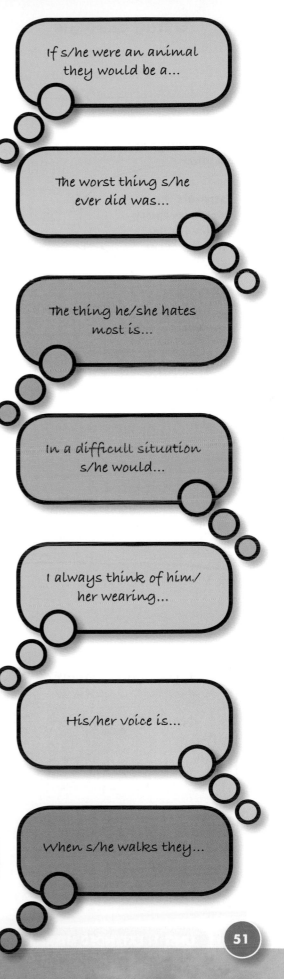

If s/he were an animal they would be a...

The worst thing s/he ever did was...

The thing he/she hates most is...

In a difficult situation s/he would...

I always think of him/her wearing...

His/her voice is...

The best thing about him/her is...

I'm his/her best friend because...

When s/he walks they...

## Using dialogue

You will need to include some dialogue in your story. The extract below gives examples of the rules for speech layout.

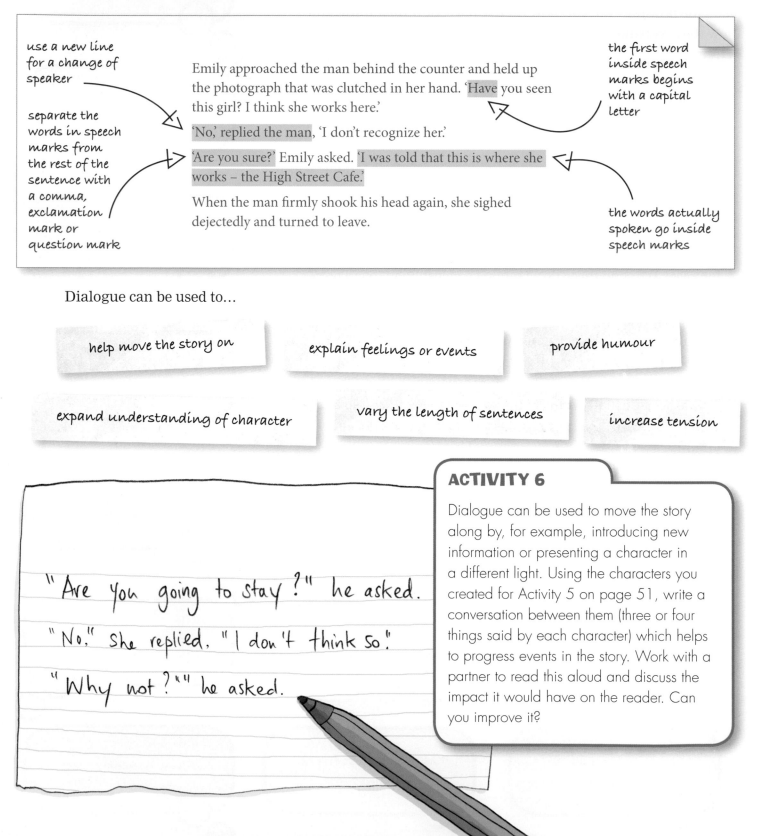

use a new line for a change of speaker

separate the words in speech marks from the rest of the sentence with a comma, exclamation mark or question mark

the first word inside speech marks begins with a capital letter

the words actually spoken go inside speech marks

Emily approached the man behind the counter and held up the photograph that was clutched in her hand. 'Have you seen this girl? I think she works here.'

'No,' replied the man, 'I don't recognize her.'

'Are you sure?' Emily asked. 'I was told that this is where she works – the High Street Cafe.'

When the man firmly shook his head again, she sighed dejectedly and turned to leave.

Dialogue can be used to...

help move the story on

explain feelings or events

provide humour

expand understanding of character

vary the length of sentences

increase tension

"Are you going to stay?" he asked.

"No," she replied, "I don't think so."

"Why not?"" he asked.

### ACTIVITY 6

Dialogue can be used to move the story along by, for example, introducing new information or presenting a character in a different light. Using the characters you created for Activity 5 on page 51, write a conversation between them (three or four things said by each character) which helps to progress events in the story. Work with a partner to read this aloud and discuss the impact it would have on the reader. Can you improve it?

UNIT 1

# Writing a story

Now it's time to put into practice the skills you have developed in this chapter by writing your own prose fiction in the activities below.

## ACTIVITY 7

You are now going to write a story called 'The Big Change'.

- To prepare, use a spider diagram or flow chart to map ideas for settings, characters and twists in the plot.
- Write your story. Remember that you need to engage your reader, so use your imagination and vary your language and sentence structure to give variety.

## ACTIVITY 8

Choose one of the activities below. They all relate to your story 'The Big Change' and will help you extend your responses to character, events and setting.

- Write a preview of a film version of your story which would appear in a newspaper or television listings magazine.
- Produce a series of emails between two of your characters about events in the story.
- Write a newspaper report about one of the events.

## EXTENSION TASK

Write a report on the work of your favourite writer. This could be for a school magazine or for a website offering older teenagers ideas for challenging reads.

# TRY THIS!

## Generating ideas

### ACTIVITY 1

Work in a group of four or five. Each person should bring in an item from home which has some importance to them; for example, a CD, a photograph or a holiday souvenir. Talk to the rest of the group about the item and its particular significance.

### ACTIVITY 2

Play 'Consequences'. Each person has a sheet of paper.

- At the top write a name (it may be a celebrity or person you know), then fold over the paper so the name cannot be seen and pass it on.
- Write the name of a different person – fold and pass on.
- Write the name of a place – fold and pass on.
- Write something one person could say – fold and pass on.
- Write a possible reply – fold and pass on.
- Open up and see what outline you have for a possible story!

## ACTIVITY 3

Take two extracts from online news reports or from two different novels – they should not be connected. Now work out a story which takes the narrative from one extract to the other in an inventive, yet logical, way.

'No one ever knew whether to believe Zac…'

'They huddled closer to the dying embers of the last fire.'

## ACTIVITY 4

One member of your group should put five or six varied items in a bag; for example, a bar of chocolate, a map or a mobile phone. As the items are drawn out one by one, the rest of the group should try to link them into a narrative.

## ACTIVITY 5

Newspapers often include very short items of about 50 words in a side column. These provide a little detail about less important stories. Develop one of these into a full-length story, either for the same newspaper, or as a short story. Clearly, you'll have to use your imagination to fill in the gaps!

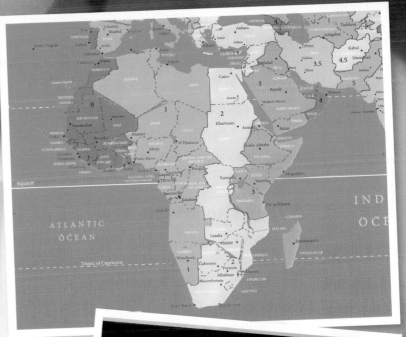

## SECTION B: IMAGINATIVE WRITING

## How can I plan for the Imaginative Writing tasks?

In the planning stages of the exercise, you may wish to work in pairs or with a group of other students. You should look at how other writers use language in order to develop your understanding of how meaning is constructed through writing. You will also be given the opportunity to practise your own imaginative writing in class to prepare you for your final assessment.

You should have plenty of time to discuss, plan and shape your responses before the Controlled Assessment. By the time you actually walk into your first assessment session, you should have a clear and detailed idea about what you are going to write.

You will need to ensure that you can write text that is accurate and fluent with thoughtfully selected content. You should be able to adapt your writing style and language to a wide range of forms, media, contexts, audiences and purposes.

## What should the style be of each response?

You should read the wording of each of the tasks carefully to determine the most appropriate **style** of writing. You should consider the following factors:

- **Form** – the genre of each piece of writing, such as prose, poetry or drama script.
- **Media** – the means of expression, such as written essay, blog or email.
- **Context** – the setting, purpose and function of the piece of writing.
- **Audience** – the readers of the writing.
- **Purpose** – the intended outcome of the writing, for example, to amuse, to advise or to persuade. A single piece of writing may have a number of different purposes.

## How much should I write?

The maximum word count for both writing tasks combined is **1200 words**. This word count should be divided equally between both parts. You will not gain any extra marks for writing more than necessary.

## What are controlled conditions?

- There will be a limit of how much time you will be allowed to spend on writing your response. You will have up to **four hours** in total for both sections.
- You can word-process the work but none of the tools on your word processor will be available to you.
- You may take some brief, bullet-pointed notes into the assessment with you but no other documentation is permitted.
- The final piece of work must be completed individually with no help from teachers or other students.

### EXAMINER'S TIPS

Remember to plan your time in your assessment so that you have time spare at the end to check your spelling, punctuation and grammar.

# SAMPLE TASKS

## Sample task 1.3

**1   PERSONAL AND IMAGINATIVE WRITING**

**(a)** Write about a time when you were younger and you felt an enormous sense of relief that something had or had not happened.

**AND**

**Either**

**b(i)** The younger brother/sister of a good friend is in a similar situation to the one which provoked your relief. Advise them on how to deal with the possible consequences of the situation in an email.

**Or**

**b (ii)** Write a speech to your class giving a humorous account of the circumstances from your more mature point of view.

**Or**

**b (iii)** Write a formal letter of complaint from somebody else who was negatively affected by the events in your story.

## Student response 1.3 (Task a)

"But that's quite alright!" laughed the lady at the door I had been dreading knocking on. "Take as much from the fruit trees as you like, we rarely pick it."

Never in my life before or since had I been so relieved to hear those words. I had been bullied and terrified into believing that I would not only be arrested by the police but probably sent to burn in hell. How had I got myself into what, for a nine-year-

*the writer uses a clear structure; we start at the end of the narrative, and read on to find out how this came about*

**Student response I.3 (Task a) continued**

old, was a pretty scary situation?

I'd never liked him, particularly. Okay, we went to the same school and it was said his mother had been a friend of my dad's in the past, but there was little or nothing that I could make of that. He was stuck-up and thought he was better than everyone else. Perhaps that was why he had trouble getting kids to go to his birthday party. Perhaps that was why I'd been given the dubious honour of now being amongst a collection of boys who'd been forced to go by our parents.

*the writer gives a concise introduction to the characters and establishes a clear narrative voice*

The one thing we did know about him was that he was terrified of their father. He and his 16-year-old brother really walked in fear of his bad temper. He'd been a war hero allegedly and expected to be treated that way, and if he wasn't he'd lash out, violently.

"You can all go into the garden and play, until tea is ready", his mother told us.

*this paragraph effectively moves the narrative on to the climax of the story*

Play, I ask you! We were being treated like five-year-olds! I walked off. It was a big garden, at least.

The elder brother came up to me.

"Get up on the wall and into the tree next door and nick some of those plums," he said. "Or I'll pull your head off!"

"No need for that," I thought. Things were getting more interesting at last.

I got up on the wall and into the tree and started hurling next door's plums down to him. Intrigued, one of the other boys climbed up on the wall and joined me. We had nearly thrown down all the fruit when...

*effective choices of vocabulary bring the narrative to life*

"Who picked that fruit?" the father roared.

"Me," I said. (Tell the truth and shame the devil, my dad always said.)

"Get down here!"

## Student response 1.3 (Task a) continued

an effective, simple closure

He grabbed me by my T-shirt and shook me.

"You're a thief! A dirty little thief! You'll rot in hell! D'you think I fought a war for scum like you? Get next door and apologise, while I call the police!"

Terrified, I walked to the front door of the neighbours' house. As I rang the bell I was shaking.

"I'm so sorry," I said, as the door opened, "I've been caught..."

Was I relieved with what I heard next! I didn't tell my parents. And I never went back there again.

brings the narrative to a crisis point swiftly and dramatically

## Student response 1.3 (Task b(i)) (extract from opening)

the tone assumes the character of the older, wiser personality effectively

Hi Kid,

So you got a mouthful and were threatened with the police; and ran home terrified and relieved all at the same time.

Know the feeling! Get over it. Do nothing until your head clears and then work out how you got yourself into the situation in the first place. You're not all bad are you? So what happened? Was it all your fault? Surely not.

When it happened to me I was nine, and pretty scared too. I thought my parents or the police would find out. Now I think I'd have preferred it if they had known, then I wouldn't have been so worried. The people who got me into that mess were just weird...

there is a clear sense of audience here

the ironic twist at the end works well

UNIT 1

## EXAMINER'S COMMENTS OCR

Relating to Student response 1.3 (Task a) and (Task b(i)).

- Both responses to Sample task 1.3 fulfil the task requirements, showing clear control of tone, language, vocabulary and style.

- Good awareness of purpose and audience.

- The first response is sophisticated and has sufficient flair to be awarded a high mark in the top band. The second is on track but needs more detail and robust development to achieve a top-band mark.

## Sample task 1.4

2 **PROSE FICTION**

(a) Write a story entitled 'Upstaged'.

**AND**

**Either**

b (i) Write the diary entries of a teacher who was directing a play based on the story. The diary should cover events from choosing the actors to the first performance.

**Or**

b (ii) Write a script for an interview to appear on a TV chat show, where one of the characters is invited to talk about events in the story.

**Or**

b (iii) Write a blog in which the central character explores his or her feelings about the experience.

## Student response 1.4 (Task a)

neat opening that sets the scene and the context for the story

She'd never wanted to be in the stupid play in the first place. But when her teacher said that she was her first choice to play one of the leading roles, Killer Queen, in 'We Will Rock You', she was so flattered that she just couldn't refuse. It wasn't that she hadn't had experience of acting before. It was just that her boyfriend Jamie was also involved. As Galileo, the leading male role. And her best friend Jasmine had been cast as Scaramouche who Jamie (Galileo, that is) falls in love with. Jasmine was her enemy in the play and, as it turned out, in real life too.

keeps the drama/ real life confusions simple and accessible

Killer Queen's big scene was in the middle of Act Two. She is told that she has been victorious over her enemies, the Bohemians. When she came off stage to a huge round of applause, there they were: Jamie and Jasmine, in a clinch behind one of the curtains.

She was gutted, totally devastated. She had been singing on stage about how successful and powerful she was when in real life she'd been completely upstaged. And by the two people she thought she was closest to.

deliberately withholds information from the reader about how this happened, which grips the reader's interest

Bad went to worse before the end of the show. With Killer Queen defeated, Galileo and Scaramouche, her now ex-best friend and ex-boyfriend, came on singing 'We are the Champions' which Jamie and Jasmine obviously thought they were, putting everything into it. She just stood there crying and then ran off the stage. The teacher was furious!

neatly drawn conclusion that links the student's writing back to the task

So after the first night, her star performance had fallen flat, and the people who had betrayed her got all the glory! Talk about being upstaged!

### EXAMINER'S COMMENTS OCR

- The reader is engaged throughout and there is a clear sense of purpose and direction.
- The use of third person and anonymity of the central character are well chosen and add to the 'gossipy' tone of the story.
- A strong middle-band response.

UNIT 1

## Student response I.4 (Task b(i))

Monday September 4th.

Great! I've got my actor to take on the role of Beth. Just need to find somebody to play Jamie and we'll have a perfect cast.

*establishes the teacher's character sparely and concisely*

Thursday September 14th.

First rehearsal completed. I'm really pleased so far. They're all so confident and enthusiastic.

Friday October 1st

*establishes and sustains an authentic chronology using dates*

A really good week of rehearsals. The actors all work really well together. I've still got to talk to the art department about helping us out with make-up and costumes. So much to do!

Wednesday October 5th

Sorted costumes; the sixth form students have agreed to help. Hope they're up to the job! Met the lead guitarist in the band that will play in the show – Mr Carter! I never knew he was a fan of rock music. Still, it's good to have his support.

*another character broadens and develops our narrator's profile*

Monday October 24th

Half-term holiday over; just three weeks left!

*reference to past events adds depth to the writing and makes the entry more convincing*

Tuesday November 7th

Final Dress Rehearsal. Went like a dream. I'm so excited. I just hope we get a good audience. Last year's play was ruined by a crying baby. The cast seem nervous but that's understandable.

*student writes well to form, recognizing that diary entries are used to record thoughts and feelings as they develop*

Wednesday November 8th

First night. What went wrong? I don't understand what happened. For some reason my lead actor couldn't get her lines out. The others tried to encourage her but then the audience started to laugh, which threw her off altogether. I feel so let down. I should never have cast her in the first place.

*dramatic note on which to end the piece*

## EXAMINER'S COMMENTS OCR

- The diary entries give the character a clear if simple personality that is developed well.
- The vocabulary is accurate but unambitious.
- The time scale gives a clear sense of structure, and the linking between 'entries' works well. Once again, a strong middle-band response.

# Unit 2

## Speaking, Listening and Spoken Language

# HOW TO APPROACH UNIT 2

## What will I cover in this unit?

This unit is divided into two sections:

- **Section A** tests speaking and listening.
- **Section B** tests how well you can analyse the use of spoken language.

## How will the speaking and listening tasks be assessed?

The speaking and listening tasks fall into three separate contexts:

- an individual extended contribution
- a group activity
- a drama-focused activity.

These tasks will be assessed by your teacher and checked by the exam board. Your teacher will choose the tasks that will work best for you.

## How will the spoken language task be assessed?

For this part of the assessment, you will be given a choice of activities; the tasks available to choose from are set by the exam board.

You can choose to look at:

- **Part A**: the study of the spoken language of a public figure (such as a politician) or an interviewer (Jeremy Paxman, for instance). This option can be linked to one of the activities in your speaking and listening assessment, using the same context or purpose adopted by your chosen figure.

**Or** you can choose **Part B** and look at one of the following topics:

- Language, Media and Technology, including study of a TV programme
- Language and Society.

As with Part A, if you opt for Part B, you will have the option to link this activity to one of your speaking and listening assessments. This means that you can base the assessment on a topic you have studied as part of your study of spoken language.

SECTION A: SPEAKING AND LISTENING

## What will the tasks be like?

Throughout your course, you will take part in a variety of speaking and listening activities. Some will take place in quite formal contexts, such as giving a presentation in front of an audience, while others will take place in more informal contexts, such as taking part in a discussion with other students.

One of the activities that you will be assessed on must have a real-life context, which means that the activity must reflect a situation that may arise outside of the classroom. For example, pitching a concept for a new video game to representatives from a software company or taking part in a debate with local residents about steps to prevent young people from loitering on the streets at night.

## What will I be marked on?

You will be marked according to Assessment Objective 1, which covers the skills listed below.

- Speak to communicate clearly and purposefully; structure and sustain talk, adapting it to different situations and audiences; use Standard English and a variety of techniques as appropriate.
- Listen and respond to speakers' ideas and perspectives, and how they construct and express meanings.
- Interact with others, shaping meanings through suggestions, comments and questions and drawing ideas together.
- Create and sustain different roles.

The three tasks combined are worth **40 marks**: each task is marked out of 40 and the three marks are then averaged. The speaking and listening tasks are worth 20% of the total marks for your English Language GCSE.

## LEARNING CHECKLIST

In this chapter you will learn to:

1 Speak clearly and to the point; adapt talk to different situations and audiences; use Standard English and a variety of techniques.

**AO1**

## Planning a presentation

One of your assessment tasks will be based on an individual extended contribution. This could involve planning a speech or presentation and then delivering it to an audience. Before giving any kind of speech, it is vital that you think about **what** you are going to say, as well as **how** you intend to say it.

As part of this, it is important to plan the structure of your speech. You could begin by focusing on three main steps, as listed below.

- **Step 1**: start clearly and purposefully by greeting your audience and introducing the title of the talk, with a line or two on what it is about.
- **Step 2**: give the key information in a clear and logical order.
- **Step 3**: conclude by summing up your ideas, thanking your audience and inviting questions.

## ACTIVITY I

Imagine that you have five minutes to persuade your English teacher to stop issuing you homework. Read the speech bubbles and answer the questions below.

**a** Which would be the least appropriate way to begin?
**b** Which would be the most appropriate way to begin?
**c** Explain your choices. Try to use the terms: 'Standard English', 'formal', 'informal' and 'colloquial'.

## EXTENSION TASK

Write the rest of the speech to your own English teacher.

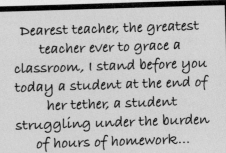

Dearest teacher, the greatest teacher ever to grace a classroom, I stand before you today a student at the end of her tether, a student struggling under the burden of hours of homework...

Good morning. My intention is to persuade you, Mr Jones, that abolishing homework would be beneficial to students' education and well-being.

Alright mate. Look, we've had enough of this homework business...

Choosing the correct level of formality for your situation and audience is important. If you get this wrong, your argument will be less effective and you risk losing marks.

UNIT 2

# Presenting persuasively

If the aim of your presentation is to persuade your audience to take a certain viewpoint, then you need to use some persuasive language techniques. The following extract is taken from a speech delivered by a Year 11 student during an assembly. It aims to persuade the audience to support the speaker in calling for a new school uniform.

"

Good morning fellow students. I am here to talk to you about the issue of school uniform. Have you ever looked in the mirror and thought, my school uniform looks really cool? How about wearing it out on a Friday night, when you meet your friends? I thought not.

If we students are forced to wear a uniform, the least the school could do is make it *remotely* fashionable. We are one of only 27% of schools in the entire country where students still have to endure a torturous tie. There are millions of schools where pupils' uniforms are modern, comfortable and, dare I say, vaguely stylish. Enough is enough: we don't expect designer gear, but this dreary, drab and dreadful dress code has to go!

## ACTIVITY 2

Read the extract and copy and complete the grid below. Explain the effect of each persuasive technique carefully.

| PERSUASIVE TECHNIQUE | EXAMPLE FROM THE SPEECH | WHY THIS IS PERSUASIVE |
|---|---|---|
| rhetorical questions | | |
| use of facts or figures | | |
| rule of three | | |
| humour | | |
| use of pronouns, such as 'I', 'you' and 'we' | | |
| exaggeration | | |

## FUNCTIONAL SKILLS TASK

FUNCTIONAL SKILLS

As a member of a local youth organization, you have been asked to produce a presentation for the leisure centre in your area. Your aim is to persuade the management of the centre to provide three new activities for teenagers. These could include after-school clubs or trips. In your presentation, remember to:
- use formal language
- briefly introduce yourself and the purpose of your presentation
- outline three new activities that you would introduce and explain why each would be popular with visitors aged between 15 and 18
- think about *how* you present your ideas; use persuasive techniques and visual aids to support your points.

## LEARNING CHECKLIST

In this chapter you will learn to:

**1** Listen and respond to speakers' ideas, perspectives and expression.

**2** Use suggestions, comments and questions to pull ideas together.

**AO1**

## Listening carefully

One of your assessment tasks will be based on a group activity. When working in a group, it is essential that you listen carefully to what other people are saying.

### ACTIVITY 1

**a** Why is it important to listen to the other members of your group?

**b** What might happen if you don't listen carefully during a discussion?

**c** Copy the spider diagram on the right. Complete it by adding other actions that help to show others that you are listening.

asking relevant questions

nodding in support of a point

**FORMS OF ACTIVE LISTENING**

### ACTIVITY 2

**a** In pairs, spend two minutes telling your partner about your weekend.

**b** As the first person talks, the second should respond as a **bad** listener might.

**c** Now swap over so that the second person talks and the first person responds as a **good** listener might.

**d** Discuss the points below.
- How did it feel to talk to a bad listener?
- How did your partner show you that he or she was listening well?

**e** While body language can help to show that you are paying attention, it is what you say in response that is real proof that you are listening carefully. Think of five questions based on what your partner told you about his or her weekend. Which questions show you were listening and why?

UNIT 2

# Responding appropriately

In your assessment you will be given marks for how appropriately you respond to what others say. This is especially important in a job interview, where you will need to give detailed answers and use formal language.

## FUNCTIONAL SKILLS TASK

You are part of the production team for the TV show *Teentastic!* and you are looking for a new presenter to host the show. Read the personal specification for this job, below:

### Personal specification

Candidates must be:

- confident at presenting to camera
- able to work well both independently and as part of a team
- fun, with a bubbly personality and an excellent sense of humour
- willing to take on a host of exciting (and potentially terrifying) challenges from fire-eating to bungee jumping!

**a** In your group, write a list of ten questions that you will ask the candidates for this job at interview.
- Use formal language in both the wording of the questions and your discussion.
- Make sure that your questions cover all of the qualities and skills identified in the personal specification.
- Create questions that require detailed responses.
- Listen to each other and attempt to involve everyone in the discussion.

**b** Swap your set of questions with another group. Use the questions to interview each other. As each person is interviewed, rate:
- how well he or she listens to the questions
- how detailed and appropriate his or her responses are.

**c** Give each candidate advice on how to improve their interview technique in order to win that job!

### LEARNING CHECKLIST

In this chapter you will learn to:

1 Speak clearly and to the point; adapt talk to different situations and audiences; use Standard English and a variety of techniques.
2 Listen and respond to speakers' ideas, perspectives and expression.
3 Use suggestions, comments and questions to pull ideas together.
4 Take on different roles during activities.

**AO1**

## Taking on a role

When you take on the role of a character, you need to think carefully about how that character thinks and feels and how he or she expresses these thoughts and feelings both verbally and non-verbally. This means that as well as considering **what** your character might say, you need to consider **how** he or she might say it.

When preparing to take on a role, decide what tone of voice is most appropriate for your character. This indicates the character's emotional state; for example, whether he or she is agitated or relaxed, unhappy or cheerful. Also consider how your character is likely to interact with other characters; is he or she likely to listen carefully and make constructive comments or be very assertive and persuasive?

### ACTIVITY I

Imagine you live in a village where there has been a proposal to hold a three-day music festival. You are going to take on the roles of various members of the village.

a Discuss who might be affected by the proposal; for example, shopkeepers, farmers, elderly people or teenagers.

b Work in groups of four. Each person decides independently what role to play and then the group improvises a conversation in the local shop or café where you discuss your thoughts about the festival proposal.

c At the end of the discussion, review your performance. Ask your peers how convincingly your character came across. Invite suggestions as to how you could improve on your role-playing.

UNIT 2

## Using actions as well as words

While you are talking in role, think carefully about your facial expressions, gestures and body language. Remember that communication isn't just about what you say. Even if you are not moving or actually saying anything, you can still maintain a role by the way you stand and move, and how much eye contact you use. An angry character might stand with a jutted chin and folded arms, and stare directly at the speaker. A conciliatory character might lean forwards, use more open body language and nod to show understanding of what is being said.

### EXAMINER'S TIPS

✔ The role of the chairperson is crucial. He or she must prepare strategies to keep the debate on track and to ensure that everyone has a chance to speak. He or she will need to limit people who speak too much and encourage people who speak less to share their views.

✔ Developing and understanding the role you are going to play is very important. Don't try to write a complete script but do make plenty of notes that you can refer to in the heat of the debate.

### ACTIVITY 2

Following on from Activity 1, imagine the village calls a general meeting to debate the issues surrounding the proposed festival. Improvise the debate with the whole class.

**a** Allocate roles, such as chairperson, festival organizer, local councillor, police representative, youth club leader and local shopkeeper.

**b** Think carefully about how to express your character's viewpoint. Make notes to help you prepare for the debate.

**c** In the debate, take turns to put forward your views, listening carefully to each other and responding to points made. When speaking, remember to emphasize what you say with appropriate facial expressions and body language to reflect your character's feelings.

**d** At the end of the debate, the chairperson should sum up the main points made and everyone should take a vote on whether the festival should proceed.

### ACTIVITY 3

Work in groups of four to improvise a local TV news item about the festival after it has taken place.

**a** The interviewer should introduce the news item and prepare questions.

**b** The three interviewees should respond to the questions in role.

**c** The interviewer should listen carefully, ask further questions to clarify points made and then summarize the event and people's opinions.

## How can I plan for my assessment?

Bearing in mind the following points will help you to carry out your speaking and listening tasks effectively:

### Identifying your audience

You will gain marks for showing that you are aware of your audience.

The audience is the person or people you are addressing or talking with. If you have a clearly defined audience, you will be able to select the most appropriate words, style and level of detail to ensure that your speech has maximum impact.

### Listening to others

Thinking about the subject matter of the tasks in advance is likely to help you to make a more confident, considered and interesting contribution in the assessment. This does not mean, however, that you should memorize exactly what you are going to say and then reel it off without pausing for breath! You need to be dynamic and be prepared to respond to comments from other speakers or questions from your audience.

To get the best marks you need to show that as well as speaking persuasively, you can also listen sensitively to what people say and recognize how they say it in order to respond to them appropriately.

### Creating and sustaining different roles

To create a convincing role, you should do some thinking beforehand and determine how your character is likely to feel about and respond to the issues that you are going to talk about. You should make sure that how you speak matches the character's perspective.

Speaking in role might involve acting out a scene in a play you have studied or a drama script you have written. The possibilities, though, are much wider than this because you do not have to necessarily work from a script; you could produce a spontaneous role-play. Remember that this is likely to be more difficult than using a prepared script!

## How long will the assessments take?

To prepare and complete each of the three speaking and listening tasks you need between three and five lessons, including some detailed discussion with your teacher before you are assessed.

## What do I need to do to get the highest grades?

Aim high! The descriptors for the top band state that you need to:

- select suitable styles showing assured use of Standard English
- choose from a broad range of vocabulary and express yourself in an engaging manner
- explain expertly, and evaluate persuasively, how you adapt language for specific purposes
- recognize and fulfil the demands of different roles in formal settings or creative activities
- initiate conversations and listen sensitively through contributions that sustain and develop discussion.

Remember, monologue is not discussion! Also, remember that you do not have to show all of these skills in one task, but across all three.

# SAMPLE TASKS

## SECTION A: SPEAKING AND LISTENING

### Section A: Speaking and Listening

### Individual extended contribution

Give a talk to your class on your hopes and aspirations for the future. These can be for you personally, for your family or for the wider world.

### Group activity

The government has decided that only ONE group of public sector workers will be given a pay rise in the forthcoming budget. In groups of seven or eight debate and decide on which group of workers should be given the pay rise. ONE person should chair the debate and the other participants should each represent a different group of workers. Example groups include:

- teachers
- water and sewerage workers
- street cleaners
- doctors
- nurses
- MPs
- police
- the judiciary (judges etc.)

### EXAMINER'S TIPS

OCR
RECOGNISING ACHIEVEMENT

These are the sorts of tasks your teacher will set in order to assess you in this unit. Your success will depend on how thoroughly you prepare beforehand. You should not focus on reading from a script but you might find it useful to have some notes to refer to.

### Drama-focused activity

One or two of the group take on the role on CID officers visiting the Macbeths' castle the night after the murder of Duncan to investigate what has gone on. The other members of the group should take on the roles of characters from the play. The detectives should interview the suspects/witnesses and decide who they wish to charge with the murder.

UNIT 2

## For sample task 2.1 (student 1)

**Teacher's notes**

Individual extended contribution

This talk engaged the class throughout, and was thought-provoking as well as humorous. The topics covered were particularly well selected.

- Confidently delivered. Student gave a talk about her own ambitions and structured this effectively.
- Student used body language and hand gestures to emphasize her points. Good eye contact sustained throughout.
- Student used sophisticated but appropriate vocabulary.
- This would fall into the top band.

Group activity

The case for teachers was argued consistently and effectively.

- Student gave complex but clearly presented arguments for paying teachers more, such us motivating staff and attracting better recruits.
- Listening skills were well demonstrated throughout: her rejection of the claims for nurses was based on a clear appreciation of what had been argued.
- Challenged others confidently on the weaker points of their arguments.
- A top-band performance.

Drama-focused activity.

Student took on the role of one of the detectives.

- Showed an excellent knowledge of the play's characters throughout.
- Portrayed the detective as thorough and strong willed. Managed to remain convincingly in character throughout.
- Student was able to react spontaneously to other characters and adapt her behaviour appropriately as events unfolded.
- Another top-band performance.

Assessment overall

Student would attain a top band mark.

## For sample task 2.1 (student 2)

### Individual extended contribution

The talk was well researched and covered a range of topics but less successful in engaging the audience throughout.

- Student played safe by sticking rigidly to detailed notes rather than using prompts.
- Talk was well paced overall, although student tended to rush in places.
- The use of visual aids to illustrate key points was helpful, though these could have been more interesting.
- Used Standard English throughout with aptly chosen vocabulary.
- This would fall into the upper middle band.

### Group activity

Relevant arguments for the case of water treatment and sewerage workers.

- Responded intelligently and positively to arguments from other members of the group.
- More repetition of key points would have added emphasis in places.
- Generally adopted an open-minded approach rather than a hostile one, which encouraged others to participate.
- Sometimes put off by interruptions and failed to conclude points effectively. A middle-band response.

### Drama-focused activity

Student took on the role of Banquo.

- Some understanding of Banquo's character and his role in the play.
- Gave appropriate responses when questioned by detectives but failed to convey the character's emotions convincingly.
- Could have used tone of voice and body language to better effect.
- Another middle band response.

### Assessment overall

This student would achieve a middle-band mark.

# HOW TO APPROACH UNIT 2

## SECTION B: SPOKEN LANGUAGE

## What will the tasks be like?

For the study of spoken English, you have a choice of activities. The tasks you do may either be set by your teachers, or adapted by your teachers from tasks set by the exam board. You can choose **either**:

**Part A**: the study of the Spoken Language of a Public Figure, which will be the study of a particular speaker or of a particular interviewer

**or**

**Part B**: the study of Language, Media and Technology **or** Language and Society.

Language, Media and Technology will include the study of a TV programme. Language and Society may include the study of gender, change over time or language in social contexts.

## Can my speaking and listening work relate to these tasks?

Yes, your Speaking and Listening work can be linked to this task. Either the individual extended contribution, group activity or drama-focused activity can use the same context or purpose (if linked to Part A), or be on the same topic (if linked to Part B) as your spoken language assessment. Your teacher will advise you on whether you will be linking these tasks.

## Is there a maximum word limit?

You must complete your Controlled Assessment work in the form of a written essay of up to **1000 words**.

**LEARNING CHECKLIST**

In this chapter you will learn to:

1 Understand how spoken language changes to suit different situations.

2 Judge the effect of your own and others' spoken language.

AO2

## Differences between spoken and written language

You might think that spoken language is the same as written language, except that one is heard and the other is visible, but you would be wrong! There are many important differences.

### ACTIVITY 1

Record a two-minute extract of speech from the radio or TV, or find one online. Transcribe the extract and compare it to a printed page from a novel. What differences can you identify between the spoken and written language used in these examples? Copy and complete a grid like the one below.

| ASPECTS TO CONSIDER | SPOKEN LANGUAGE | WRITTEN LANGUAGE |
|---|---|---|
| How many people are involved? | | |
| Does the writer/speaker pause or hesitate? | | |
| Can you identify evidence of non-verbal sounds? | | |
| Does the speaker/writer communicate in full sentences? | | |

## Planning and creating speech

You could think of written language as **static** or unchanging, whereas most everyday spoken language is **dynamic**. This means it is created instantly, in response to immediate events. As most spoken language forms part of conversation, it is produced as a joint effort, while writing is usually a solitary activity. People generally produce spoken language without much chance to plan. The less planning there is, the more spontaneous the language will be. Although you can correct yourself, you can't actually delete the spoken words.

### ACTIVITY 2

List three spontaneous spoken interactions you have had in the last few days. For each, note:

- how many people were involved
- whether there were other listeners, who were not speaking
- how much planning was involved; use a scale of 1–5, with 5 representing the most spontaneous.

UNIT 2

# Public and private speech

In this chapter, you will consider one type of spoken language: the spoken language of a public figure. Most public figures have what they say broadcast in the media, such as on the radio, TV and websites, as well as any speaking they might do at venues open to the general public. Their audiences are therefore often large and diverse, so they have to tailor what they say to engage as many people as possible.

One of your assessment tasks for this unit is to study the spoken language of either a particular speaker or interviewer. You will need to think carefully about how this type of spoken language differs from everyday conversational talk.

## ACTIVITY 3

Read the speech bubbles below. With a partner, decide which might be spoken by a public figure on a public occasion and which might be spoken by family or friends in a private setting. Note that some might be both. Give reasons for your decisions, considering aspects such as:

- level of formality
- audience appeal
- choice of vocabulary
- use of pronouns.

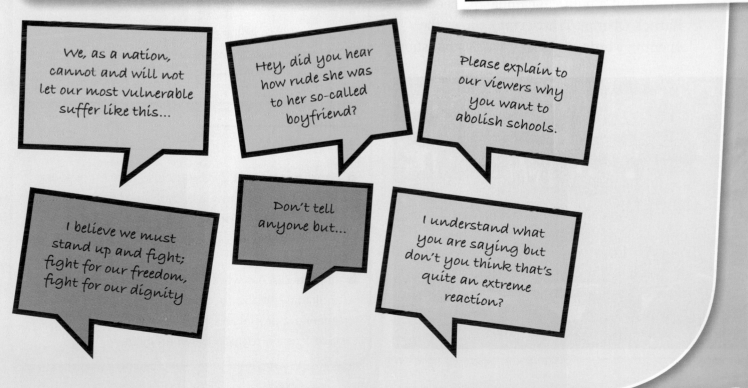

We, as a nation, cannot and will not let our most vulnerable suffer like this...

Hey, did you hear how rude she was to her so-called boyfriend?

Please explain to our viewers why you want to abolish schools.

I believe we must stand up and fight; fight for our freedom, fight for our dignity

Don't tell anyone but...

I understand what you are saying but don't you think that's quite an extreme reaction?

## Rapport and audience

All public speakers need to think carefully about their audiences and establish a suitable rapport or relationship with them. Someone giving a public speech, such as a politician or campaigner, needs to first acknowledge the audience by greeting them and then try to gain their goodwill by making them feel appreciated. For example, the speaker will often try to convince the audience that he or she is 'on their side'.

In contrast to a political speaker, an interviewer needs to speak on behalf of the audience, asking questions and seeking information from the interviewee. An interviewer might acknowledge this wider audience, making the listeners feel valued. In addition to this, he or she also has to establish a relationship with the interviewee.

Look at the transcripts of spoken language above, to the right. Transcript 1 is the opening of a political campaign speech by Barack Obama. Transcript 2 shows the opening words of a host on a TV chat show.

**1**

'Let me begin by saying thanks to all you who've travelled, from far and wide, to brave the cold today.

We all made this journey for a reason. It's humbling, but in my heart I know you didn't come here just for me, you came here because you believe in what this country can be.'

**2**

'Good evening. Thank you for joining me again for another chance to put today's most pressing questions to the country's leaders. I hope that together we can explore the controversial action being taken on our children's schools. Please join me in welcoming the Minister of State for Schools and Learners...'

### ACTIVITY 4

Annotate a copy of Transcript 1 to show how Barack Obama establishes a rapport with his audience. Consider the following aspects:
- use of the pronoun 'we'
- appreciation of the audience
- being modest about his own status
- reference to high ideals.

### ACTIVITY 5

**a** Look at Transcript 2. Using close references to the speech, explain how this chat-show host:
- establishes a rapport with his audience
- prepares to establish a positive rapport with his interviewee.

**b** In pairs discuss what the interviewer could do to maintain a good rapport with his guest as the interview progresses. Think about what could damage the rapport between them.

## Pace, pauses and body language

To make an effective speech, a speaker not only has to plan **what** to say, but also **how** he or she intends to say it. Here are some unspoken or **non-verbal** aspects of speech-making that you need to consider:

- pace (how quickly or slowly you speak)
- use of pauses
- volume (how loud or quiet your speech is)
- eye contact with your audience
- body language (gestures; the way you stand)
- movement (whether you are static or move around).

In your response, you should consider how these factors are likely to affect the impact of what the speaker says. Slowing down the pace of speech, for example, will allow the audience to hear the words more clearly and can therefore be used to add emphasis. Speeding up the pace can add more energy to what is being said and can create a sense of hype and excitement.

Pauses can be used in a similar way. A carefully placed pause after a point will give the audience more time to reflect on its significance. Fewer pauses will make the speech more fluid.

Movement and body language can be used to aid meaning but too much can be distracting. Deliberately limiting movement can lend more gravity to what is being said and make a speaker seem more definite or sincere.

> 'How many people do you know who love football? I'm betting that everyone knows someone with a passion for "the beautiful game". You may even have the passion yourself. Football is more than a game, it's a national obsession. Football transcends class and gender; you will find fans from all walks of life. It is a sport that binds us together as a country…'

### ACTIVITY 6

In small groups, take turns to present the opening of a short speech. You could write the opening yourself or use the transcript below left, which focuses on the popularity of football.

**a** On your first turn, deliberately underperform one of the non-verbal skills listed on the left. For example, you might speak too quietly, too fast, or use too many pauses. The rest of the group will then try to identify the flaw in your speech.

**b** On your second turn, try to present the speech to the best of your ability. The rest of the group will then comment on aspects you did well.

**c** For each positive aspect they identify, ask them to explain how this helped to enhance the meaning of what you said.

# Rhetoric: the art of speech-making

The overall sound and rhythm of a speech can have a powerful impact on an audience. Many famous political speakers are able to convey emotional power through careful control of tone and pace.

'Rhetoric' is the Greek term for the art of speech-making. Public speakers use various rhetorical devices to add impact to their words. These devices can consist of choices of vocabulary, sound effects or structural patterns. Here are some common **rhetorical devices**:

- **emotive words**, for example: 'our brave lads' rather than 'the soldiers'
- **rhetorical questions**, for example: 'Do you find this acceptable?'
- **balanced phrases**, for example: 'to work and to live'
- **antithesis** or placing opposite meanings together, for example: 'Let us shape our hopelessness into new hope'
- **repetition**, for example: 'We will stand up, we will fight, we will win.'
- **tripling** or groups of three, for example: 'Friends, Romans, countrymen'
- **onomatopoeia**, for example: 'the people are clamouring for justice'
- **alliteration**, for example: 'a tapestry of talents'.

## ACTIVITY 7

Read the transcript of the opening of Obama's nomination speech on page 83. Identify examples of rhetorical devices and comment on the effect upon the audience. For example, do the devices stir up emotion, make something memorable, incite action or give emphasis? Or do they have a different impact?

## EXAMINER'S TIPS

OCR
RECOGNISING ACHIEVEMENT

If you identify rhetorical devices in your assessment task, remember that you must also explain **why these devices** are used and **what effects** they create.

UNIT 2

Here is the full opening of Barack Obama's campaign speech for Democratic nomination for US President, from February 2007.

'Let me begin by saying thanks to all you who've travelled, from far and wide, to brave the cold today.

'We all made this journey for a reason. It's humbling, but in my heart I know you didn't come here just for me, you came here because you believe in what this country can be. In the face of war, you believe there can be peace. In the face of despair, you believe there can be hope. In the face of a politics that's shut you out, that's told you to settle, that's divided us for too long, you believe we can be one people, reaching for what's possible, building that more perfect union.

'That's the journey we're on today. But let me tell you how I came to be here. As most of you know, I am not a native of this great state. I moved to Illinois over two decades ago. I was a young man then, just a year out of college; I knew no one in Chicago, was without money or family connections. But a group of churches had offered me a job as a community organizer for $13,000 a year. And I accepted the job, sight unseen, motivated then by a single, simple, powerful idea – that I might play a small part in building a better America.

'My work took me to some of Chicago's poorest neighbourhoods. I joined with pastors and lay-people to deal with communities that had been ravaged by plant closings. I saw that the problems people faced weren't simply local in nature – that the decision to close a steel mill was made by distant executives; that the lack of textbooks and computers in schools could be traced to the skewed priorities of politicians a thousand miles away; and that when a child turns to violence, there's a hole in his heart no government could ever fill.'

## Techniques of interviewing

In your assessment task you may choose to study a particular interviewer, so you need to be aware of how he or she manages the timing of participating speakers.

In an interview the participants take turns to speak. This may seem straightforward, but it is often quite complex. Listen to any interview with one or more interviewees and think carefully about:

- who speaks first or sets the **agenda**
- who has the most, or longest, **turns**
- who interrupts and tries to take over the **floor**
- whether the speakers **overlap** and talk at the same time.

One way to control turn-taking is through question and answer exchanges. The type of question can affect the rapport between the interviewer and the interviewee. Here are some key question types:

- **closed question**: invites a 'yes' or 'no' answer
- **open question**: invites an unpredictable response
- **leading question**: already implies something
- **tag question**: seeks confirmation.

### ACTIVITY 8

**a** Decide what types of questions these speech bubbles contain, referring to the list above.

> That's right, isn't it?

> What do you think of it?

> Have you seen it?

> Have you stopped taking bribes?

**b** For each question type, identify one positive and one negative effect that might result from using it. For example, an open question might prompt an imaginative response, but the answer you get could also be quite vague.

## Sir Michael Parkinson

Sir Michael Parkinson is one of the most famous interviewers on TV and radio in the UK. Starting out as a journalist, he moved to TV and radio and became hugely popular, interviewing almost 1000 of the world's most famous people.

Although he has now retired, many of Parkinson's interviews are available to watch on the Internet and in particular on his own website. Some of Parkinson's most famous guests included Nelson Mandela, Will Smith, Gwyneth Paltrow, Sir Paul McCartney, David Beckham, Simon Cowell, Tom Cruise, Sanjeev Bhaskar and David Tennant.

### ACTIVITY 9

Watch at least two of Parkinson's interviews. In pairs, make notes on or discuss the following aspects:

- the way Parkinson introduces his guest to the audience before he or she appears
- how he greets his guest, physically and verbally
- the use of humour, particularly early in the interview, to establish a rapport
- how Parkinson conveys a sense of respect for his guest
- Parkinson's body language, such as eye contact, hand gestures and facial expressions, and the effect on the interviewee
- the style of questions that Parkinson asks, in order to evoke the fullest and most interesting responses from his guest
- how the questions usually allow the guest to reveal a chronological account of his or her life and/or career
- how Parkinson rounds off the interview and thanks his guest.

### ACTIVITY 10

Over the years, Sir Michael Parkinson developed a very specific style and formula for his interviews. Why do you think they were so successful? Consider these viewpoints and add your own.

> The interviews were revealing, but in a friendly non-judgemental way.

> Parkinson didn't hog the limelight, unlike so many other chat-show hosts.

> Everything was carefully researched and the questions were well-planned.

### EXAMINER'S TIPS

Different interviewers have different styles of interviewing, often favouring certain question types over others. They are likely to adapt this style to suit particular guests or the subject matter of the interview. Watching or listening to as many interviews as you can will help you to familiarize yourself with a range of styles.

# TRY THIS!

## Changing personas

### Playing a role

You may think that every person has a fixed identity, but the word 'person' actually derives from the Greek 'persona', meaning mask! During the course of a day, one person may in fact play many different roles, depending on the situation he or she might be in. People usually manage this without thinking. In the next activity, you will see how we can consciously create different personas in our spoken language.

To help you answer Activity 1, **either**:

use a pack of playing cards, with the Ace, King, Queen and Jack cards signifying a high status, going down to number two representing the lowest status.

**or:**

choose a situation from the list below. You are:

- a school inspector who is writing a report on the class
- the Head Teacher sorting out a discipline problem
- a journalist from a local newspaper who wants to write an article about exam results
- a student from the class with an authorized reason for being late
- a student from the class who has already been late several times.

### ACTIVITY I

Each member of the class tries the following in turn.

**a** Take a playing card or pick a situation from the list, and leave the classroom. Enter as if you are arriving late, after the class has started. Speak, without giving away who you are or why you have come, and take a seat according to your chosen status or situation. The rest of the class will then try to guess the situation or which status card is held.

**b** For each person you observe, explain how you decided upon his or her status or situation based on the person's speech and behaviour.

## Pause for thought...

You will notice that people use sounds like 'er', 'erm' and 'um', when they speak. These are known as **filled pauses**. They might show that the person is unsure of what to say next, but they can have different effects. This often depends on where you pause and how long the pause is.

For example, if you begin to speak with a very short 'er', you may seem unsure of yourself. If you make the 'erm' longer, you may seem more assertive. If you move the 'um' into the middle of what you are saying, the effect will be different again.

I wanted to, er, ask you a favour.

er, I wanted to ask you a favour.

erm, I wanted to ask you a favour.

I, um, wanted to ask you a favour.

I wanted, erm, to ask you a favour.

um, er, I wanted to, er, ask you, erm, a favour.

### ACTIVITY 2

a Take on the role of a character and decide on an opening sentence. You could choose one from the examples on the right.
b Write down the sentence and memorize it exactly.
c With a partner, or in a small group, recite your line three times, experimenting with the length and position of filled pauses.
d Take feedback on the effect the changes had on the persona you portrayed.

Good evening everyone, I'd like to say a few words.

I propose a vote of no confidence.

Excuse me, I was sitting there.

Could you lend me five pounds?

Is this the right room for enrolment?

Mrs Scott said she wanted to see me.

I'm sorry I didn't come yesterday.

# Language, Media and Technology

## LEARNING CHECKLIST

In this chapter you will learn to:

1 Understand how spoken language changes to suit different situations.

2 Judge the effect of your own and others' spoken language.

**AO2**

## Recording and broadcasting speech

Modern technology surrounds us with a constant stream of pictures and sounds. Whether it is on the radio or TV, on mobile phones or MP3 players, you probably hear more spoken language through technology than in live, face-to-face talk.

Spoken language used in the media is recorded and broadcast to the public. Most face-to-face talk you experience every day, however, will not be recorded and is likely to remain private. People adapt their ways of talking depending on the situations they are in. For example, if people know that what they say is being recorded, they tend to think more carefully about what they say.

## ACTIVITY 1

In pairs, discuss examples of spoken language that you have listened to recently via media and technology. Decide whether each example is **scripted** (written down), **unscripted** or a mixture of the two. Record your ideas in a grid, like the one started below. Consider media sources such as TV, radio, podcasts and the Internet.

| SCRIPTED | UNSCRIPTED | MIXTURE |
|----------|------------|---------|
| TV drama, e.g. Hollyoaks | TV talk shows, e.g. Jeremy Kyle | TV reality shows, e.g. The Apprentice |
| radio… | | |

In this chapter you will study unscripted spoken language and how it varies in the media, through the use of technology and in face-to-face situations.

# Editing broadcasts

'Reality' shows are popular on TV. Despite their name, they do not simply record 'real' talk. Most programmes mix different types of spoken language from a variety of speakers. Here are some different types of talk you might find in a reality show:

- **voice-over**: scripted commentary from an unseen presenter
- **voice piece to camera**: a regular presenter delivering semi-scripted or planned speech
- **interview**: presenter and guest(s), where the presenter has questions prepared
- **conversation**: unscripted, but edited, talk between two or more people
- **vox pop**: edited highlights from various people talking on a single topic.

With the use of technology, editors are able to influence how spoken language is received. They choose the most interesting or controversial parts and put it into sequence to make an entertaining whole, like a collage. Although music, sound effects and visuals are not part of your English Language study, they all contribute to the overall effect of spoken language on the viewer or listener.

## ACTIVITY 2

Choose a reality TV programme that interests you. As you watch it, do the following:

**a** note down the different types of spoken language used

**b** for each type of spoken language that you identify, note how much planning you think it needed.

The grid shows an example taken from *Big Brother*, which was one of the first reality shows to become popular on UK TV. In this show, contestants agreed to live in a house for three months and to be filmed continuously. Contestants were then voted out or 'evicted' by the general public each week. The last one left in the house at the end of the series was the winner.

| BIG BROTHER EVICTION NIGHT | DEGREE OF PLANNING (1–10) |
|---|---|
| title music and visuals | 10 |
| voice piece to camera | 9 |
| voice-over 1 | 10 |
| conversation 1 | 4 |
| voice-over 2 | 10 |
| conversation 2 | 5 |
| interview | 6 |

# Formulaic language

Many media programmes use set language patterns that are repeated in each episode and even within episodes. This may take the form of expressions that are used time and time again in specific situations. For example, words used by reporters to open and conclude news stories. Some TV shows also feature **catch phrases**. These short, repeated expressions are an important way of creating a recognized brand or identity. Some phrases eventually become used in spoken language outside the programme, often for comic effect.

Formulaic language, including catch phrases, helps to make programmes memorable and distinguish them from each other. Some catch phrases are always accompanied by a distinctive animation, sound effect or image to reinforce the brand in the audience's mind. For example, in the BBC's reality TV show *The Apprentice*, Sir Alan Sugar's catch phrase 'You're fired' is always accompanied by his pointing finger.

## ACTIVITY 3

With a partner:

**a** write down three situations where formulaic language might be used on a TV or radio programme

**b** for each situation, discuss why this type of language might be used

**c** jot down as many catch phrases as you can think of from programmes that you have seen or heard

**d** discuss whether these catch phrases are used in spoken language outside the programme.

## ACTIVITY 4

**a** Imagine you work for a TV channel and you are helping to design a new TV show. With a partner, think up a name, a catch phrase and a suitable logo for one of the programmes suggested below:

- a challenge show where teams must make useful items out of other people's rubbish
- a nationwide competition to find the best amateur DJ
- a show following the progress of teenagers at a sports academy, competing to win a year of free professional coaching.

**b** What kind of formulaic language might be used in the show you have created? Give examples.

UNIT 2

# Conventions in conversation

Conventional comments exchanged by two people often follow a predictable pattern. For example, if someone says 'hello', it would be strange not to respond with a similar greeting. People also often try to match the level of formality, so 'Good morning' is likely to be echoed with 'Good morning', but 'Hi' would prompt a more informal response.

To the right are some common pairs of spoken exchanges for apologies, thanks, invitations and compliments.

Question and answer pairs are predictable in the sense that an answer is generally expected to a question. However, some questions are worded **openly** to invite a variety of responses, while others are **closed**, inviting short, very predictable responses.

## ACTIVITY 5

**a** Decide whether the questions listed below are open or closed.

'Lovely day, isn't it?'

'Is there any chance of lending me a fiver?'

'Have you got a minute?'

'Do you like my new haircut?'

'Why didn't you tell me she was coming?'

'What are you doing this weekend?'

**b** Write down possible responses to the questions. Compare your answers with a partner. Are there any similarities?

**c** Explain how the wording of some questions invites a fuller response than others.

### EXTENSION TASK

**a** Watch a video of a TV show involving an interview between a presenter and a guest. Pause the video each time the presenter asks a question. Try to predict the guest's response. Note the number of open and closed questions.

**b** Discuss how this use of language suits the particular situation. Think about the participants and the purpose of the interview as well as audience and setting.

## Hostile questioning

The appeal of some reality TV programmes relies on people who are willing to reveal their weaknesses in front of presenters and the viewing public. Presenters may ask some straightforward questions simply to seek information, but other questions may be loaded. **Loaded** questions imply a judgement or try to provoke a certain reaction. This type of question is often used to try to reveal the underlying attitude of the speaker. Hostile questioning is also present in some news or political interviews.

### ACTIVITY 6

Identify the loaded questions here. What might the speaker be implying in each case?

'How much money did you say you lent her?'

'Do you think that constant fighting is good for your child?'

'Why don't you leave him?'

'What do you call yourselves?'

'So, do you really think you can compare yourself to...?'

'How do I know that you are telling the truth now?'

'Didn't you stop to consider the consequences?'

### EXTENSION TASK

Watch a video of a show that involves hostile questioning. Transcribe the questions and identify which ones are loaded.

'How well did you know each other before you got married?'

'How do you think he feels about your previous offences?'

## Power and status

The rapport between a professional broadcaster and a member of the public is likely to be unequal. The presenter tends to have the upper hand because it is his or her show, but some members of the public manage to maintain an equal footing. They can do this by using assertive strategies, such as:

• **partial agreement**: 'you have a point... but...'
• **reframing the question**: 'it is not about leaving him...'
• **calmly restating the point**: 'I *have* considered the consequences.'

Note that these strategies are always more effective than shouting or becoming aggressive.

# Linked responses

It is not only question and answer pairs that can be predictable. In many conversations in the media, one person will respond to a statement by repeating key words; for example, '50,000 spectators!' or by encouraging further explanation, using a phrase such as 'Tell me more.'

## ACTIVITY 7

**a** Read the transcript below and identify all:
  - question and answer exchanges (note that punctuation has been left out)
  - statement and response exchanges.
**b** Summarize the strategies used by the therapist to respond to the other person's talk.

### Transcript of part of a therapy session

**Client**: men are all alike

**Therapist**: in what way

**Client**: they are always bugging us about something or other

**Therapist**: can you think of a special example

**Client**: well my boyfriend made me come here

**Therapist**: your boyfriend made you come here

**Client**: he says I'm depressed much of the time

**Therapist**: I'm sorry to hear that you're depressed

**Client**: it's true I'm unhappy

**Therapist**: do you think that coming here will help you not to be unhappy

**Client**: I need some help, that much is certain

**Therapist**: what would it mean to you if you got some help

**Client**: perhaps I could learn to get on with my mother

**Therapist**: tell me more about your family

Linguists (experts in language) believe that most conversations follow set patterns and conventions. This has been tested by programming a computer with the 'rules' of conversation and asking volunteers to participate in a dialogue with it.
The above 'therapist' was in fact a computer!

The computer displays conventions of conversation, such as question and answer exchanges, matching the level of formality and reassuring the speaker that it has understood statements by repeating words that the speaker has used.

## ACTIVITY 8

Although the computer successfully mimics the conventions of speech, in real life these rules are sometimes broken. How might the following scenarios affect the conventions of speech:
  - one speaker mishears the other speaker
  - one speaker is over-familiar with the other
  - one speaker is uncomfortable with the topic of conversation.

# Features of unscripted language

When people are talking without a script or without much planning, their language is likely to include certain recognizable features. These features are so common you probably don't notice them.

Here are some examples:

| FEATURES OF SPONTANEOUS LANGUAGE | EXAMPLES |
|---|---|
| repetition | 'I will add, I will add' |
| incomplete sentences | 'it was just… I don't know' |
| backchannel behaviour (where the listener uses sounds as feedback, rather than words) | 'yeah/mmm/right' |
| fillers | 'y'know/I mean' |
| vague language | 'sort of/or whatever' |
| intensifiers | 'just/really/ideally' |
| reporting speech | 'he says he's happy to be involved' |
| clichés | 'over the moon/sick as a parrot' |
| headers (beginning a comment with reference to the main subject) | 'that new goalie, he's brilliant' |
| tails (referring to the main subject at the end of a comment) | 'he's useless, that referee' |

## ACTIVITY 9

Read the transcript of a radio show on page 95.
**a** List the speakers involved and estimate the degree of planning for each. Use a scale of 1–10, where 10 represents the highest level of planning.
**b** Identify features of unscripted language in the transcript.

### EXTENSION TASK

Record another radio phone-in feature and carry out a similar analysis of it.

## EXAMINER'S TIPS

If you choose to study this topic you will need to show how people adapt features of spoken language to 'achieve specific outcomes in different situations'. The more effectively you do this the more marks you will get.

This invented radio phone-in is based closely on programmes on local radio. It includes the following:

- presenter promoting the programme
- presenter introducing the caller
- interaction: presenter's speech
- interaction: caller's speech
- sound effects (SFX), including a pre-recorded jingle
- presenter's links to other speakers
- speaker presenting the weather, traffic and news.

**Presenter**: It's 6pm and we're live with a round-up of this week's football action.

Your number one football forum; it's Football Frenzy (SFX) on Radio Newport.

This is yours truly, Gareth Newman, waiting for *your* calls every weeknight from six 'til seven. Call 0123 456789 or text us on 1123.

Radio Newport – your favourite radio station.

We'll be bringing you all the latest news from the terraces, plus reports from news and travel every 15 minutes...

But first let's go to Lisa with the latest traffic news. Lisa?

**Lisa**: Hi Gareth. Yes... er, traffic's flowing pretty steadily in the city centre, but there's a bit of a hold-up between Junctions 9 and 10... It's very slow, so avoid it if at all possible.

**Presenter**: We'll bring you an update in a few minutes time, after the news.

Meanwhile... we've got, uh, Danny on line one. How're you doing, Danny?

**Danny**: Not so bad, Gareth.

**Presenter**: So, what's your point today?

**Danny**: Well, erm, I'm just hoping the back four put in a better performance tonight, really.

**Presenter**: Yeah, I can see what you're saying... I quite like Turner, to be honest.

**Danny**: Yeah. Yeah, you've definitely got a point there... I mean, obviously.

**Presenter**: OK, thank you. That's Danny, a United fan from Moorside...

We've got literally hundreds of texts coming in but let's get back to the lines.

This is Gareth Newman. Good evening.

**Sue**: Hi Gareth, this is Sue.

**Presenter**: Nice to hear your voice again, Sue. What've you got to say?

**Sue**: I think we need to give the lad a chance to, um, show what he can do, you know?

**Presenter**: Well, that's a matter of opinion, of course...

**Sue**: Like the manager said, 'he's new, give him time to settle in'.

**Presenter**: Sue, thank you for your call. Remember, keep your calls coming in!

## Language change

Trends in spoken language are always changing. Have you noticed, for example, that 'like' is a word that is being used more and more frequently in conversation? It is generally used as a **colloquial** word, which means it is more suitable for informal conversation than for formal speech or writing.

'Like' is often used colloquially to add emphasis or as a filled pause. For example: 'It was a fair result, like'; 'it was, like, awesome'; 'what he said was, like, really out of order'. One of the most recent changes in the use of the word is how it is used to introduce direct speech (see the speech bubble above). Other common ways of introducing speech are, 'I said... she said...' and the colloquial 'I goes... she goes...'.

Researchers think that the growing popularity of the word 'like' originally began in America, particularly among young females. This is just one small example of the way spoken language has changed in recent years.

> So I was like, 'You're so totally not gonna wear that today', and she was like, 'Dude, I am'.

## ACTIVITY 10

**a** Conduct a survey among your classmates. Who uses the word 'like' in conversation? Are you aware of it in your own speech or others'? What is the effect of it on listeners?

**b** Research the use of 'like' in written language on the Internet. Type 'I was like' into a search engine and note the number of hits. Now try phrases such as 'I was like hey/whoa/huh'. This should give you examples of where 'like' is being used to introduce speech.

## ACTIVITY 11

**a** Think of three other words that you use but people of a different generation, such as your teachers, parents or grandparents, don't use.

**b** Look each word up in a dictionary and if this word is listed, note down the different meanings connected with it.

**c** Note which uses are Standard English and can be used in a formal way, and which are listed as 'informal', 'colloquial', 'slang' or 'non-standard'.

## Variation in spoken language

Spoken language varies hugely. No two people speak in the same way and people rarely speak exactly the same way twice. But the variation is systematic: it follows recognizable patterns and conventions.

An effective speaker adapts his or her language use, according to the situation he or she is in. The speaker will be aware of these important factors:

- **audience**: who am I speaking to/who is listening?
- **purpose**: why am I speaking/what effect am I trying to achieve?
- **genre**: what type of talk is it: chat, phone call, radio programme, audition or something else?

### ACTIVITY 12

You can present a different version of yourself – a different persona (see page 86) – by adapting the way you speak.

**a** Choose one of the situations listed below or invent your own, but remember that it needs to be linked to media or technology:

- an audition for a talent show or inclusion in a reality TV show
- a telephone call to your employer, explaining that you are sick
- a video presentation about revision techniques for your school website
- a telephone call to a friend you have met only once before
- an email apology to your best friend for an argument the day before.

**b** Role-play the opening words.

**c** Get feedback from others on your use of language and its effectiveness in the situation you have chosen.

### EXAMINER'S TIPS

You need to show how spoken language is influenced by changes in communities, societies and technologies. To practise this, listen to conversations from different time periods. For example, you can find clips from past TV programmes online. Use what you have learnt in this chapter to help you to identify and explain the differences you find.

**A02**

## LEARNING CHECKLIST

In this chapter you will learn to:

1 Understand how spoken language changes to suit different situations.

2 Judge the effect of your own and others' spoken language.

## Private talk

The spoken language you will study in this chapter is private, in the sense that it is between people who are in the same place, at the same time, and who know each other. Unlike spoken language used in the media, private talk is not usually recorded or broadcast to the general public.

People might use private spoken language in any of the following situations:

- in the classroom
- in the playground or sports field
- at a social event or family setting
- in the workplace
- at home.

## Spontaneous talk

Most private talk is unscripted or **spontaneous** because the people are reacting to each other, or events, in an immediate way. Private talk is also usually **informal**, as most of it takes place casually between friends, family or colleagues. This relaxed form of speech is likely to include a variety of features such as those listed on page 94.

However, not all private talk is entirely spontaneous or informal. In some situations, it is necessary to speak in a formal manner, because the relationship with the other person is not close or equal. Alternatively, there might be a serious topic to discuss that requires a particularly careful or sensitive approach. In these cases, people may take time to think about what they are going to say before the dialogue takes place.

### ACTIVITY 1

Make a recording of two different conversations; for example, one could be between students at school; the other could be between family members at home. (Ensure you have permission to make the recordings first!)

**a** Listen back to the conversations and take notes on each one. These should include:

- how evenly turns are taken to speak
- the use of non-verbal interjections; for example, grunts, hums and other sounds that signify some sort of response
- the choice of vocabulary; for example, whether it's age-related, repetitive or jargon
- where the speakers challenge or support each other
- how information is shared
- how instructions are given and/or received.

**b** Discuss the differences and similarities between the conversations. How does each reflect the context (place and situation) in which it took place?

## Formal and informal language

If we are in a formal situation we are likely to use formal language. The grid to the right shows some differences between formal and informal talk.

## Informalization of language

Nowadays, the use of informal spoken language is becoming more wide-spread. Even in some formal situations, such as political speeches, features of informal language are becoming more acceptable, even desirable. Using accessible, informal speech might give the speakers an advantage, such as appealing to a wider, younger audience. For example, political leaders such as Barack Obama and Gordon Brown often include colloquial, informal phrases in their speeches, such as 'I get it' and 'Yes, we can'. Tony Blair used the phrase 'cool Britannia' to promote his new Labour image to younger voters in the 1990s.

| FORMAL SPOKEN LANGUAGE | | INFORMAL SPOKEN LANGUAGE | |
|---|---|---|---|
| standard grammar | "Wouldn't you say?" | dialect or slang | "dontcha?/ innit?" |
| standard vocabulary | "...because it was impressive" | abbreviations or vague phrases | "cos it was pretty cool" |
| full sentences | "I plan to go to university." | unfinished utterances | "I'm going to... you know..." |
| formal terms of address | "Mr Carter" | use of first names, nicknames or no name | "Ronnie / hey mate" |

### ACTIVITY 2

With a partner, choose two situations involving two people: one formal, the other informal. You could use the situations illustrated on the right if you wish. One shows two friends discussing a pair of damaged trainers in a shop. The other shows somebody returning a pair of damaged trainers that he has purchased.

a Improvise a short scene for each situation using language that you think is appropriate.

b Show your role-play to another pair, asking them to identify which is the formal and which is the informal scene.

c Ask them whether they think the language use is appropriate in each.

# Spoken language in a family situation

Examples of private spoken language seem chaotic when written down, compared to the orderly turn-taking of interviews.

A written record of spoken language is known as a **transcript** of speech. Here is a transcript of a family conversation between a mother, Anna, her son Jake, and her American daughter-in-law, Kerry. The conversation takes place as they are driving home after a trip to an indoor snow slope. The use of underlining shows which words are emphasized.

**Jake**: I'm quite proud of myself for not crashing. I thought somebody had come off at the very bottom 'cos when we got there this toboggan [*laughs*] flew past, fractionally missed about three people and crashed into the bottom. Then Kisa pulls up behind me and goes "That's your Mum's" [*laughs*]

**Kerry**: Terrible business [*laughs*]

**Anna**: It wasn't though. I was still on my toboggan.

**Kerry**: Oh, were you still?

**Jake**: 'cos you did roll a bit.

**Anna**: I know, I was just sort of sitting there really.

**Jake**: Nobody was braking.

**Anna**: The man said "Are you alright?" and I said "Yes".

**Jake**: I think they keep a couple of toboggans on the side 'cos otherwise there's no way for you to get down [*laughs*] It's like "oh well you've just had a nasty fall so we want you to walk down this slippery hill" [*laughs*]

**Anna**: There's no other way to get down. Yeah, so he handed me back my glasses and my hat

**Jake**: ...and a fresh toboggan 'cos yours nearly killed people [*laughs*]

**Kerry**: Oh, terrible business [*laughs*]

**Anna**: Why didn't they say that at the safety talk?

**Jake**: [*laughs*] What, "Don't let go of your toboggan, whatever you do"? [*laughs*]

**Anna**: No, "You can steer to the right but don't just yank the thing or you'll turn it over".

**Kerry**: Kinda common sense?

It is not only words that convey meaning in spoken language. The way a person **sounds** can be very revealing: their volume, tone of voice and pace of speaking all combine to create a specific impression. People also use expressive sounds, such as laughter, sighs, and utterances like 'mm' or 'oh', to show the speaker they are paying attention.

Silent gaps in the middle of talk are known as **pauses** and these can be very important in spoken language. Sometimes people pause simply because they need to take a breath or have time to think of what to say next. However, pauses can have other functions. For example, they might signal that the next word is:

- important
- unexpected
- sensitive.

## ACTIVITY 4

Read the transcript opposite aloud, twice, in groups of three. Vary the tone of voice and pace with each reading to convey a different atmosphere each time. Try taking out the laughter or adding expressive sounds to enhance the effect. Without changing the words, try to convey two of the following scenarios:

- one of the characters is angry about what happened
- two of the participants don't get on very well
- one of the participants is bored with the conversation
- one of the participants is nervous about speaking.

## ACTIVITY 3

Look closely at the transcript on page 100.

**a** What features of this transcript suggest that it is part of an informal conversation? You should consider vocabulary, tone, abbreviated words and expressions.

**b** When do the participants laugh and why? What does this tell you about the rapport between them?

## EXAMINER'S TIPS

To gain high marks in this unit you need to show 'perception and originality' when analysing how speech changes to suit different contexts. This means that you need to look closely and think carefully in order to uncover points that are not immediately obvious.

## ACTIVITY 5

Copy and complete the grid below, using the transcript on page 100 for reference.

**a** Note where you think a pause might be effective for each speaker.

**b** Explain what function you think each suggested pause might have.

| SPEAKER | ADD EXTRA PAUSE TO... | FUNCTION OF PAUSE |
|---------|----------------------|-------------------|
| A |  |  |
| K |  |  |
| J |  |  |

# Language and social power

In some conversations, you may sense that one person has more power. In addition to **what** they say, this could be evident in the amount they say and the vocabulary they choose. Remember that these things are variable. For example, a powerful boss may use few words but be firm and decisive; an effective teacher may talk a great deal, using humour, variation of tone and questioning techniques.

The balance of power in a conversation can be affected by many different factors, such as age, occupation, gender and situation. People can be powerful in some situations and not in others; for example, a politician may not feel powerful at a toddler's birthday party.

Using powerful spoken language does not necessarily mean giving orders in a raised voice. There are other equally effective ways of taking control, such as using persuasion, suggestion, encouragement or expressing sympathy. Silence and long pauses can be powerful tools during a conversation. They can express control or anger, or they can be a way of withholding information. Often, if a speaker says very little, what they do say has more impact.

Is it time to go home yet?

## ACTIVITY 6

In pairs, role-play two conversations where one person shows more power than the other. Think carefully about how you might convey this through features of spoken language.

- First, decide on a situation that is fairly conventional; for example, a judge addressing his or her courtroom.
- Second, choose a situation where stereotypes are reversed, so the balance of power is unusual; for example, a judge has to apologize to a neighbour for scratching his or her car by accident.

## ACTIVITY 7

Imagine passengers facing delays at an airport. Which message from the airline do you think would be most effective and why?

Thank you all for your understanding and patience during this delay.

Please stop complaining and harassing the staff. We are doing our best.

## Language and gender

The link between language and gender is **controversial**, which means it causes a lot of argument. Below are some key questions.

- Do males and females have a different way of using language?
- Could this explain problems in relationships?
- Is this the reason why fewer women get top jobs?

### ACTIVITY 8

The grid below contains some common claims about language and gender.

With a partner, discuss whether you agree or disagree with each of the aspects listed. Think of examples to illustrate your views.

| ASPECTS OF SPOKEN LANGUAGE | FEMALES | MALES |
|---|---|---|
| quantity of talk | more than men | less than women |
| preferred topics | emotions, people | facts, sports and cars |
| vocabulary | precise and subtle to convey shades of meaning | more general except in areas of speciality, e.g. technical knowledge |
| grammar | exclamations/questions tagged to the end of statements, for example: "You don't want that, do you?" | statements, orders |
| pronunciation | high rising tones for statements | flat or falling tones |
| taboo language | avoid coarse words | swear a lot |

On the right is a transcript of a conversation between two people about making a music compilation. The use of underlining indicates words emphasized by the speaker.

### ACTIVITY 9

**a** Do you think the speakers in the transcription are male, female or indistinguishable?

**b** With a partner, compare and explain your decisions.

A: You didn't need to do <u>that</u> much work. I appreciate it, but I think you didn't need…

B: … Yeah, well, I think the next time you need me to do it <u>I</u> won't be doing it.

A: Yes you will do. Don't say it like that. I'm saying I appreciate it – it's lovely. It's just why did you do four versions then? I'm not annoyed, I'm just curious.

B: Do you wanna give me a break or do you wanna trust me?

A: I did. I'm just curious, I'm just having a conversation with you.

B: You say that but it sounds like you're complaining…

## Giving instructions

The classroom is a place where many instructions are given out to students. This is a basic requirement for any kind of teaching or training. You might expect the spoken language of teachers to be therefore full of orders such as, 'Do this.... /Listen to this... /Read the passage...' These verbs are known as **imperatives**. However, the majority of teachers use a variety of spoken strategies to be effective. These strategies include replacing imperatives with:

- questions
- statements
- exclamations.

For example, 'Would you like to start reading from page 6?' is a question and another way of saying, 'Read from page 6'.

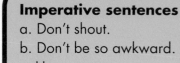

1. Have you finished?

2. You don't need to shout.

3. What a helpful comment!

**Imperative sentences**
a. Don't shout.
b. Don't be so awkward.
c. Hurry up.

### ACTIVITY 10

**a** Match each speech bubble above to its equivalent imperative. You might think of the imperative as the 'real' order that the teacher is giving.

**b** What has the imperative been replaced with in each case? A question, a statement or an exclamation?

**c** Why do you think a teacher might use this strategy? What impact do you think each strategy is likely to have on a student?

### ACTIVITY 11

The same strategies can be used outside the classroom: in the workplace, at home or with friends. Imagine four different situations where you might need to persuade someone to do something for you and where you would need to ask them carefully; for example, you want a parent to give you a lift or you want to borrow money from a friend.

Copy and complete the grid to the right.

| SITUATION | INDIRECT SPOKEN LANGUAGE | DIRECT MEANING |
|---|---|---|
| You come home late one evening with some friends | 'You're making a lot of noise.' | 'Be quiet.' |
|  |  |  |

## Spoken language in the classroom

You will have had years of experience of using spoken language in a classroom situation, but you may not have analysed this in detail. Listen carefully in a couple of lessons and think about the following questions.

1 What proportion of the lesson is taken up by the teacher talking?
2 What proportion of the lesson is taken up by the students talking?
3 Who contributes most in terms of spoken language: female or male students?

## Language and occupation

We adapt our spoken language according to what we are doing and who we are with. Some jobs have their own specialized vocabulary or **jargon** which can be baffling to outsiders. For example, the jargon used by solicitors will be very different to that used by DJs or research scientists or sports physiotherapists.

Some jobs not only have their own jargon, but staff are trained to speak in a certain way, particularly when interacting with customers. In sales jobs, for example, employees may be trained to use persuasive techniques that are likely to have a positive influence on customers.

### ACTIVITY 12

Choose a topic that interests you; for example, sport, fashion or music.
**a** List the specialized jargon that 'outsiders' may not be familiar with.
**b** Exchange your list with a partner and talk about the terms you recognize and those you are unfamiliar with.
**c** Think of two advantages and two disadvantages of using jargon in speech.

Read this extract from a training manual for telesales staff.

| 1 | Customer name | Use softly, e.g. 'Thank you for calling, Mr Jones'. |
|---|---|---|
| 2 | Your name | 'My name is Narinder Ray. How can I help you?' |
| 3 | Your details | 'Our free phone number is…' |
| 4 | Summarize | 'I will put the revised bill in the post and…' |
| 5 | Understanding | 'Is that alright/clear, Mr Jones?' |
| 6 | Further help | 'Is there anything else I can help you with today, Mr Jones?' |
| 7 | Goodbye | 'Goodbye' should be said clearly rather than clipped 'Bye' followed by a quick phone down. |
| 8 | Phone down | Let the customer put the phone down first. |
| 9 | Tone | Avoid sounding aggressive or too passive. |

### ACTIVITY 13

With a partner, role-play a telesales conversation, using some of the guidance given above. Before you start the conversation decide the company's name and business. If possible, record the conversation for comment and analysis later.

### EXAMINER'S TIPS

A top grade analysis of speech will distinguish carefully between features that reflect the speaker's personality and features that reflect the role he or she plays professionally; for example, a teacher or a police officer.

# PREPARING FOR UNIT 2

## SECTION B: SPOKEN LANGUAGE

### How will my work be marked?

You will be marked on Assessment Objective 2, which tests the skills below.

- **Understand variations in spoken language, explaining why language changes in relation to contexts.**

  We all have different registers of speech, depending on who we are speaking to and what our purpose is. The language you use at home when communicating with your family is likely to differ from the language you use at school when speaking to your teachers. People use different language for different **purposes**; for example, to persuade others, to give instructions or to entertain each other.

  People also use different language in different **situations**; like attending a job interview or chatting to a friend on the phone.

  Why do people say the things they do? What reactions do they expect and what reactions do they actually get? A careful study of spoken language will reveal details of character, intention and feeling.

- **Evaluate the impact of spoken language choices in your own and others' use.**

  We are all influenced by the way other people speak, whether this results in trying to emulate them, ignoring them or trying to speak in the opposite way. For example, how would you want to sound if you were trying to encourage people to give money to charity? What language choices would you make if you wanted to end a relationship? The way you speak might be influenced by language that you have heard in the past: someone you saw on a news programme; lines from a character in your favourite soap.

  You may relate one of your speaking and listening activities to your study of spoken language.

## How will the task be presented?

Whether you decide to write about the Spoken Language of a Public Figure, Language, Media and Technology or Language and Society, your task will be contextualized by your teacher, who will give more specific information about points that you should cover.

You may take notes into your assessment for reference. You are also allowed to take in unannotated transcripts of speech for reference.

### EXAMINER'S TIPS

- ✔ A good way of preparing for this assessment is to try to think carefully about people you hear talking on the radio or that you see and hear talking on TV. As well as people in the media, listen to people communicating socially and in more formal situations.

- ✔ Think about the way that people say things as well as what they are saying. For example, take note of their tone, vocabulary and style of speaking.

- ✔ Ask yourself how the conversation might differ if the context were different; for example, talking to just one good friend; talking in front of a studio audience; talking to the police.

- ✔ Try to become conscious of how you change your own language depending on the situation you are in and who you are talking to.

# SAMPLE TASKS

## SECTION B: SPOKEN LANGUAGE

**Sample task 2.2**

### Section B Spoken Language

### Part A: The Study of the Spoken Language of a Public Figure

**A1 A study of a particular political speaker selected from Winston Churchill, Barack Obama or Nelson Mandela.**

The study of spoken text and commentary could consider:

- how spoken texts are structured and the key features of speech

- how the speaker establishes a rapport with the audience

- how language is used to create impact (and what the impact is); for example, diction, register, rhetorical devices

- the use and impact of timing pace/pause, movement (if the text is shared visually) and other features specific to the text

- an evaluation of the ways in which you may have attempted to reproduce the key features in your own Speaking and Listening presentation.

### Extract from speech by Winston Churchill
#### 4th June 1940

We shall go on to the end, we shall fight in France, we shall fight on the seas and oceans, we shall fight with growing confidence and growing strength in the air, we shall defend our Island, whatever the cost may be, we shall fight on the beaches, we shall fight on the landing grounds, we shall fight in the fields and in the streets, we shall fight in the hills; we shall never surrender, and even if, which for a moment I do not believe, this Island or a large part of it were subjugated and starving, then our Empire beyond the seas, armed and guarded by the British Fleet, would carry on the struggle, until, in God's good time, the New World, with all its power and might, steps forth to the rescue and liberation of the old.

### EXAMINER'S TIPS

**OCR** RECOGNISING ACHIEVEMENT

The student who wrote the response on the next page chose to study a speech made in 1940 by the British war leader Winston Churchill. The final part of this speech is printed on the left. In consultation with your teacher, you will be able to choose which speaker to focus on from the options provided in the task description.

UNIT 2

### Student response 2.2 (to Winston Churchill's speech)

I thought this was a very powerful speech. Churchill cleverly succeeds in doing two things at once. He warns his audience of the terrible struggle lying ahead of them, urging them to fight and defeat the enemy and yet he also suggests a safe and secure alternative if they don't, by encouraging the USA to come to Britain's aid. He starts by mentioning "the end" but doesn't actually reveal what this might be until the last lines with "the New World". He makes the speech turn on a dramatic assertion, which is enclosed by punctuation so that it is almost in parentheses: "which for a moment I do not believe". This links the warning to the persuasion. The scenes of fighting he depicts actually follow the course of a successful rather than a defeated invasion "on the beaches... in the hills".

*comments effectively on the structure of the text; an example of the way the punctuation works would help here*

He establishes a strong rapport with his audience (both the MPs in the House of Commons and the public listening to the radio) by repeating the word "we" ten times in the first half of the speech. This denotes solidarity, commitment and a shared sense of purpose in trying to do everything possible to repel a hated enemy. In a broader sense a rapport with the USA is established by his use of the phrases "in God's good time" and "the New World". The alliteration in the former emphasizes the suggestion that God has a plan for the USA to intervene and that it is his will that it should do so.

*good analysis of how the speaker develops a rapport with the audience*

The latter puts Americans, very flatteringly, in a context of being the embodiment of the pioneers of political and religious freedom who had followed Columbus to the Americas centuries previously.

*a complex but well-expressed sentence*

## Student response 2.2 continued

There are many other examples of effective diction and register here. "Our Island" adds to the sense of collective resistance; the repetition of the verb "shall" reinforces the sense of an indomitable spirit and the alliteration of "subjugated and starving" emphasizes both Britain's need of American support and the bloodiness of what the British people might have to put up with.

*good focus on rhetoric but could say more about diction and register*

The speech sweeps forward in one sentence to the seemingly inescapable conclusion: things may be awful now but God will send America into the war to save us.

*acute observation about timing and pace*

When we had our Case Conference for the speaking and listening assessment I found that I was giving a long list of examples, preceded by the same phrase "did you know that he also…" to make my point about excluding the badly behaved student.

*a clear and confident link with own speaking and listening, which could be developed further*

## EXAMINER'S COMMENTS OCR

- This answer shows insight and engagement with the text: there are some touches of originality.

- It shows a measure of analytical understanding: the choice of references is apt.

- The student makes some thorough and sensitive comments on the detail of the speech.

- There is a strong awareness of the context of the speech.

- This answer is likely to fall into the top or upper band.

**Sample task 2.3**

**Part B: Language, Media and Technology**

**B1 A study of the Spoken Language of sitcoms**

When analysing these texts, consider:

- the use and misuse of different registers and how this helps to convey a particular setting or atmosphere

- the language involved in acting out a role

- the use of colloquial English and non-standard grammar

- the use and impact of timing, pace/pauses, body language and other specific features of the spoken texts

- the influence of the genre on the spoken texts you are studying

- an evaluation of what you have learnt about spoken language in this context

- an evaluation of the ways in which you may have attempted to reproduce key features in your Speaking and Listening presentation.

## EXAMINER'S TIPS

- ✔ The student whose response begins on page 112 decided to study the sitcom *Fawlty Towers* (broadcast on BBC Television 1975–1979). An extract from the first episode is included on the following page.

- ✔ Remember that you will be able to take copies of speech transcripts into the Controlled Assessment with you for reference, as long as they are not annotated.

## Extract from the *Fawlty Towers* episode 'A Touch of Class' (1975)

**Mr Wareing:** We're halfway through…

**Basil:** Thank you so much.

**Mr Wareing:** Yes, but…

**Basil:** This is Lord Melbury's table, you see.

**Mr Wareing:** What?

**Basil:** Lord Melbury. When he stays with us he always sits at this table.

**Mr Wareing:** Well why did they put us here?

**Basil:** Ah, an oversight… on my wife's part. I'm so sorry. He's only just arrived, you see. Would you mind?... Polly!... Would you help these people to that table? Thank you, thank you so much.

*The family get up, very unwillingly. Mrs Wareing is particularly slow.*

**Basil:** Come on! Come on! Thank you.

*Melbury enters.*

**Basil:** Ah, Lord Melbury! Do please come this way… your lordship… I have your table over here by the window… as usual… just here.

---

### Student response 2.3 (extract from opening)

*effective opening, setting out the main focus of the response*

The language used by the main characters in Fawlty Towers helps to create a distinct hierarchy between them, which works to comic effect. Basil views himself as 'top dog': in the episode 'Communication Problems' he states proudly, 'I am the owner, madam', and his constant bossy treatment of Manuel shows this attitude. We frequently hear Basil shouting "Manuel!" and then giving him an order or a telling-off, with Manuel quietly replying "Si, si!". However, this is reversed with Sybil as Basil immediately agrees to do what she says, which shows her dominant position over him. Sybil's stern utterances of "Basil!"

*point backed up effectively with further linked example*

## Student response 2.3 (extract from opening) continued

*[margin annotation: shows awareness of how body language adds to the meaning of spoken langauge]*

frequently cause him to flinch, which contrasts with his dominance over Manuel. Her use of language demonstrates her calm control in most situations ("I'll deal with this") and highlights Basil's flustered, impatient approach ("Get on with your meals!"); it is clear that she is the real leader.

*[margin annotation: considers how the character's language changes depending on who he addresses]*

Basil's tone and use of language adjusts depending on who he is addressing. With guests he swings between rudeness and over-politeness. In the episode 'A Touch of Class', he is very rude to the Wareings and is super polite to Melbury. He doesn't allow Mr Wareing to finish a sentence, interrupting constantly, saying "Thank you so much" and "Come on, come on". When Wareing asks him a perfectly reasonable question: "...why did they put us here?" Basil responds by blaming Sybil: "an oversight... on my wife's part" in which it's clear he's lying; and then enlists Polly to do the dirty work.

*[margin annotation: clear and well-founded comments, but sticks to a literal interpretation of the text]*

*[margin annotation: starts to show how language is affected by changes in society]*

The next moment, we see a complete contrast as Basil goes back to fussing around Melbury, "Ah! Lord Melbury... do please come this way... your lordship...". His tone of voice becomes much friendlier. The way that Basil adjusts his language creates parody and farce. In 1975 this depended on understanding class differences: more than three decades on they aren't relevant.

*[margin annotation: links to own speaking and listening work]*

In our class's radio phone-in I was the presenter. I found I had to work out where I wanted the show to go by changing the way I spoke to each of the callers...

## EXAMINER'S COMMENTS OCR

- A reasonably developed response that offers some interpretation of how features of spoken language can be used to create comic effects.

- The student comments on some details of the chosen sitcom with well-selected and relevant quotations.

- The penultimate paragraph requires more consideration. It begins well but is not developed.

- This is a middle-band response. To get more marks, this student needs to demonstrate a wider understanding of how different features of spoken language can be used for effect.

# Unit 3

## Information and Ideas

## HOW TO APPROACH UNIT 3

### What is covered in this unit?

Like Unit 1, this unit tests your reading and writing skills but it uses different types of texts. The reading texts in this unit are non-fiction and the writing is informative, linked to the non-fiction texts.

### How will I be assessed?

You will sit an exam, with unseen text and writing tasks, which will count for 40% of your English Language GCSE. It will be marked and assessed by examiners.

There are no word limits on what you write, although you only have two hours to complete the exam. The golden rule is to put the **quality** of your response before its **quantity**.

### What will be in the exam?

The exam is divided into two sections; which are worth 40 marks each.

- In Section A you will be given two passages of unseen material to read; one will be a non-fiction piece and the other a media piece. They will be on a related topic, theme or issue.
- In Section B you will have a choice of two tasks. Each task will specify a different form (for example, a letter or a talk) and different audiences for the writing.

There are separate papers for the Foundation tier (from grade G up to grade C) and the Higher tier (from grade E up to grade A*) in this paper. Your teacher will guide you on which tier is most appropriate for you to enter.

## What will I be assessed on?

In this section you will marked according to Assessment Objective 3, which covers the skills listed below.

- **Read and understand texts, selecting material appropriate to purpose, collating from different sources and making comparisons and cross-references as appropriate.**
  This means that you will be marked on how effectively you can select relevant material from what you have read. Much of what you read will be relevant but not all of it. You will not get extra credit for making the same point more than once.

- **Develop and sustain interpretations of writers' ideas and perspectives.**
  This focuses on how well you can show that you understand the writer's ideas and perspective. Your interpretation of the non-fiction text must describe the information it contains and explain which segments of it are relevant to the task; and in the media text, to explain the writer's point of view and the ways he or she seeks to direct you to it.

- **Explain and evaluate how writers use linguistic, grammatical, structural and presentational features to achieve effects and engage and influence the reader.**
  This requires you to analyse the language and structural choices the writer has made and the effects that these have on you, the reader.

**AO3**

## LEARNING CHECKLIST

In this chapter you will learn to:

1 Understand texts, choosing parts that are relevant to certain ideas and comparing texts where necessary.

2 Explain how writers use language, style and form to create specific effects on the reader.

## Reading non-fiction texts

This chapter is about non-fiction texts that you see in everyday life, such as advice leaflets in a doctor's surgery or persuasive articles in a holiday brochure. Writers deliberately craft their texts to have an effect on you, the reader; for example, to persuade you to do something or to buy something, to entertain you or to give you information. Read the following extract from a leaflet advertising an adventure park.

alliteration makes the name memorable

Bored with the sofa? Ready for new challenges? Looking for a day out with friends?

a rhetorical question challenges the reader to act

### THE OUTRAGEOUS OUTDOORS CENTRE

### WHAT WE OFFER

Outrageous Outdoors is the best place to find adventure and exhilaration. Our centre includes: a first-rate zipwire, high speed go-carting, abseiling, climbing, caving, quad biking, assault courses, arcades and water sports.

list shows large variety of activities to appeal to different people

99% of visitors who visited last year rated their day at the centre as 'fantastic'.

statistic reinforces the point that visitors enjoy themselves.

'I've never had a better day with my mates. There is so much choice.' *Gurpreet, 15*

'The races, competitions and team games mean that everyone gets involved.' *Mohammed, 16*

opinion reinforces the sociable aspect of the activities

### TRAINED INSTRUCTORS

Our fully trained and experienced staff will provide you with all the guidance you need to make the most of our activities.

### TRY SOMETHING NEW

The Outrageous Outdoors Centre is the perfect place to learn a new sport with all the support you need. So why not try something new today?

'I went for the climbing, zipwire and the quad biking. I had never climbed before but the instructors were brilliant. The quad biking was awesome and made a great end to the day. We'll be back!'
*Jason, age 15*

emotion adds personal interest

a quotation confirms visitor satisfaction

09867 43576959
www.outrageousoutdoors1000.co.uk

UNIT 3

The flow diagram below shows the thought process that writers go through when creating their texts.

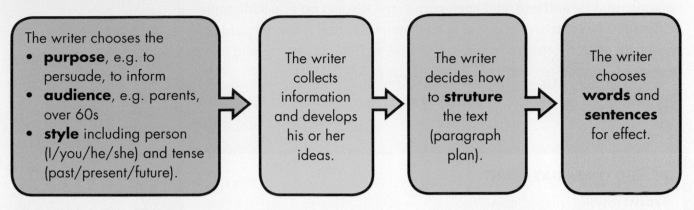

| | | | |
|---|---|---|---|
| The writer chooses the<br>• **purpose**, e.g. to persuade, to inform<br>• **audience**, e.g. parents, over 60s<br>• **style** including person (I/you/he/she) and tense (past/present/future). | The writer collects information and develops his or her ideas. | The writer decides how to **struture** the text (paragraph plan). | The writer chooses **words** and **sentences** for effect. |

## Persuasive techniques

When constructing a persuasive text, authors often include certain features or techniques. These features can be remembered using the mnemonic: A FOREST.

| TERMS | DEFINITIONS |
|---|---|
| Alliteration | Words that begin with the same sound (e.g. fantastic features). |
| Facts | Points that can be proven. |
| Opinions | What someone thinks or believes. |
| Repetition and Rhetorical Questions | Repeated words or phrases, and questions to make one think but do not require an answer. |
| Emotion | Words and ideas that stir strong feeling in the reader. |
| Statistics | Figures to support ideas or arguments (e.g. 92% of people believe exercise is good for you). |
| Three | The power of <u>three</u> or more things in a list. Lists can show options, give examples or emphasize reasons. |

### ACTIVITY I

**a** Write down examples of the persuasive techniques that the writer uses in the leaflet on the previous page. Use the mnemonic A FOREST to help you. Choose different examples to those highlighted by the annotations.

**b** For each example that you find, explain how the technique works to persuade the reader.

### FUNCTIONAL SKILLS TASK

Look in a local newspaper for adverts for activities, hobbies or groups that you would like to try. Read each advertisement carefully and find three techniques that persuade you to try out the activity; these could include specific vocabulary, images and layout.

FUNCTIONAL SKILLS

## Structure, sentences and words

The structure of a text is important. A good, clear structure has a specific opening, middle and end, and each paragraph focuses on a specific topic or theme. The structure of a text is its framework, and it should guide the reader through a logical sequence of text. A writer's sentences and words flesh out the structure with the detail of the text.

Read the email below. The writer is trying to persuade a friend to go to a gig.

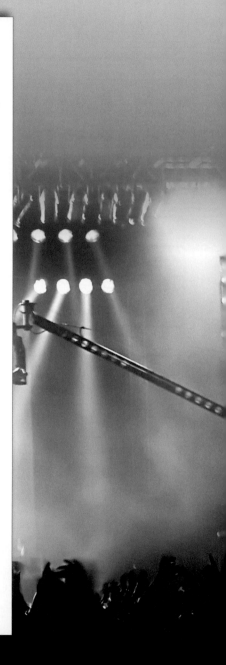

**RE: GIG ON FRIDAY NIGHT**

**From:** me@musicworld.com
**To:** you@musicworld.com

Hi,

What are you up to at the moment? It's been a while since I've seen you. We should get together to catch up.

Have you ever been to the exhibition centre in town? It's massive. They have all sorts of events there; it's an ideal place for music. In fact, this Friday there's something on. The exhibition people have invited our favourite band. They will also have loads of other music: new bands and bands looking to be signed. Before and after the gig, we can get our CDs signed. Haven't you always wanted to see them up close?

If you're worried about what your parents will say, don't be. It's an event for under 18s. There will be security and no random people or tickets will be allowed in. I can get my dad to give us a lift and pick us up.

And don't worry about the cost! It's only a fiver each and Dad giving us a lift will save us money. There will be CDs and t-shirts on sale but we don't have to buy any of that. You can come round to mine and eat before we go. Then we'll only have to worry about drinks. It'll be so hot in there with all of those people (the atmosphere will be wild!); we'll only need water.

Remember how good the gig in Birmingham was? There were so many people, the music was live and loud and the experience was better than anything we'd been to before. What if we had missed it? Let's not miss this one!

Let me know as soon as you can so that I can buy the tickets. Say hello to everyone for me. Looking forward to seeing you,

One of your best mates!

The email on page 118 has a clear structure and the writer has thought carefully about sentences and word choices. Do you think the writing is effective? If this friend had emailed you, would you have agreed to go to the gig?

## ACTIVITY 2

**a** Think of a title for each of the paragraphs in the email.

**b** Name two things the writer thinks may put her friend off going to the gig.

**c** Do you think her **counter-arguments** are effective? Explain your answer with close reference to the structure of the text.

## FUNCTIONAL SKILLS TASK

Find leaflets for different events in your local area – perhaps from the library or tourist information centre. How successful is each one in fulfilling its purpose?

- What persuasive techniques have been used?
- Look at the information provided in each leaflet – is it all essential? Is anything important missing?
- Does it appeal visually or would it be easily overlooked among other leaflets?
- Of the leaflets you have collected, which one do you think is the most effective? Which event would you attend?

## ACTIVITY 3

Write a paragraph to explain how the writer makes the email persuasive. Consider:

- vocabulary and phrasing
- tone
- sentence structure
- types of question
- punctuation.

Back up your answer with close reference to the text.

## EXTENSION TASK

Find a review of a live performance, such as a music concert or a play. You could look online or in a newspaper. Compare the structure of the review with the email on page 118. Consider:

- how information is sequenced
- which details the writers choose to emphasize and how they achieve this
- how the writer opens and closes the text.

## EXAMINER'S TIPS

When writing about the structure of texts, make sure that you link your observations about structure to the purpose of the text you are studying. Remember to comment on how effectively the structure works to help convey meaning.

## Formality and style

At home and with friends, most people chat informally. However, there are times when it is necessary to speak more formally; for example, when attending a job interview or when making a complaint about bad service. It is the same when you write. Writers have to think carefully about how formal they need to be to suit their purpose and intended audience. Read the letter below:

16th July 2011

Miss Laura Gwent,
16 Butterfield Street,
Chauchester
CS36 SDL

Mr Greggs,
VClothes,
10 Winterfield Road,
Chauchester
CS45 7XL

I am writing to apply for the position of shop assistant at VClothes as advertised in the Local Herald on 10th July.

I am currently studying eight GCSEs at Crossworth School, Chauchester. I am a reliable and trustworthy student who is looking forward to gaining more work experience. I attended two weeks of work experience at Bravo Superstores last month showing that I have the skills required to be a shop assistant. My employer particularly commented on my conscientious approach and punctuality.

At school, it is predicted that I will pass all of my GCSEs. Furthermore, I am studying catering which means that I have learned to be polite and approachable when working with customers during our catering events.

My interests show that I have a sense of humour and can meet a challenge. I am interested in TV comedies and climbing.

I am in the last year of school and hope that a weekend job at your store will help me in my ambition to work in retail.

Finally, please do not hesitate to contact me for further details or references.

Yours sincerely,

Laura Gwent

## ACTIVITY 4

a Which words or phrases help to create the formal tone of the letter? Look up any words that you do not understand.

b Look at the structure of the letter. Write one or two words to explain what each short paragraph is about.

c The main purpose of this letter is to give the reader information. How well do you think the writer does this? Explain your answer with close reference to the text. (Think about whether the style is concise or wordy, polite or too personal, etc.)

## ACTIVITY 5

Job advertisements in newspapers are often brief, particularly if the writer has to pay for every word printed! Writers usually want to get their information across quickly and clearly. How do the writers achieve this in the adverts above? Consider:

- imperatives (verbs that give commands)
- sentence length
- use of adjectives and adverbs.

## ACTIVITY 6

**a** Choose one of the advertisements below and write a letter of application. (You can invent the addresses and names.) Use ideas from the letter on the previous page to help you. Remember to use formal words.

**b** Peer assessment: Swap your letter with a partner.

- Check that the your partner's letter includes formal words. If any informal words are used, suggest formal alternatives.
- Decide whether you would offer your partner an interview on the basis of their letter. If not, explain why and suggest ways to improve the letter.

---

**Dog walker wanted**. Once a day, five times a week, 20 minutes per day. Must love dogs. Must be reliable and trustworthy. Two references essential.

---

**Café seeks confident person** to take orders at the counter. Must be able to greet people enthusiastically and politely! Hours negotiable. **£8 per hour.**

---

AMATEUR DRAMATICS group seeks teenagers to take on roles in our new production. Hard work but excellent experience for would-be actors. Auditions early next month.

---

GARDENING NEEDED. Flexible hours. No experience required. Learn on the job. Equipment provided. £7 per hour.

---

## FUNCTIONAL SKILLS TASK

- In groups of three or four, collect several adverts for weekend jobs in your local area. You could look online or in your local newspaper.
- You are going to write a draft letter of application for one of the jobs advertised. In your group, choose the advert that is the most interesting.
- Each member of the group should write their own letter of application. Select and include information that is relevant and use an appropriate structure, tone and style.
- Read the letters as a group and discuss which is the strongest application and why.

## Promotional texts

Some pieces of writing have a range of purposes. Imagine you are looking at a website selling computer games and you come across a survey. The survey has been set up by a software development company that wants to create one of two new games. The company has written a promotional text for each of the new games and wants to know which game has widest appeal. It will develop the most popular game. These promotional texts give information as well as try to persuade the reader that the game is worth buying.

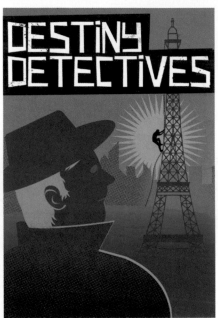

### DESTINY DETECTIVES

You will take the role of one of five detectives as you travel through the most famous cities in the world. Explore each living, breathing city on foot or in one of a range of authentic vehicles, speaking to residents and uncovering clues. Each suspect will have their own story to tell – but don't be fooled by appearances!

Every decision you make, every word you speak will have consequences on how the game pans out. You will need to think carefully, act quickly and make the most of your environment to be successful.

The cities have been re-created in amazing high definition, with a music score from Hollywood's top composers. This is more than just a game, this is an experience you will never forget!

### REAL RACING

Real Racing: the next best thing to being behind the wheel. You don't even need to earn the best car. We'll throw it in at the beginning. Start with a fantasy car. Then trash it in an obstacle-filled track. Now, start all over again…

With so many cars to choose from, wreck, and choose again, you won't get bored with this racer. Customize your car from the suspension up, or select one of over 50 pre-configured rides. Then tear up the track in over 20 breathtaking locations.

Take to the road in cities including London, New York, Paris and Tokyo. You can even drive on the same tracks as Lewis Hamilton. Have your friends join in the action with team-based or competitive online matches. Your game, your rules.

More restless and rapid than the rest: Real Racing.

Often the writers of promotional texts will use a number of different writing techniques and devices. Here are some of the techniques commonly used in this type of writing:

alliteration

common, informal phrases

rhetorical questions

exaggeration

jargon

imperatives (verbs that give an order)

punctuation for emphasis

lists

repetition

## ACTIVITY 7

Copy and complete a grid like the one below.

| TECHNIQUE | EXAMPLE |
|-----------|---------|
|           |         |

**a** Find examples of the techniques listed above in the promotional texts on page 122.

**b** Choose three techniques from those you have identified and explain why the writer decided to use them. What effect do you think he or she wants to create? Refer to the text in your answer. For example:

*Alliteration is used to make the title of the game memorable and emphasizes the word 'real'. 'Real Racing' makes the reader imagine that the game will be as good as racing a real car.*

## EXTENSION TASK

Write your own promotional text, using some of the techniques in the example texts.

Choose one of the following products to promote:

- a book containing short biographies of famous sportspeople
- a film about a teenager who finds a winning lottery ticket
- a computer game about exploring an alien world.

## EXAMINER'S TIPS

Remember that many persuasive and promotional texts will be seeking to persuade you to adopt a particular point of view. Some may be aimed at encouraging the reader to act in a certain way, to support a cause or to spend money. You will be rewarded in the exam for showing that you are able to read between the lines and get to the truth of what the writers of these texts are setting out to do.

# Reviews

When reading a text, it is important to think about the **way** it is written and **how effective** it is rather than just focusing on what it is about.

In this section you will look at film reviews. Effective film reviews usually include personal opinion, technical language specific to films (such as 'close-up' or 'screenplay'), brief comments on the plot, the acting and actors, and recommendations about who might enjoy the film.

Read the following user reviews from a film website.

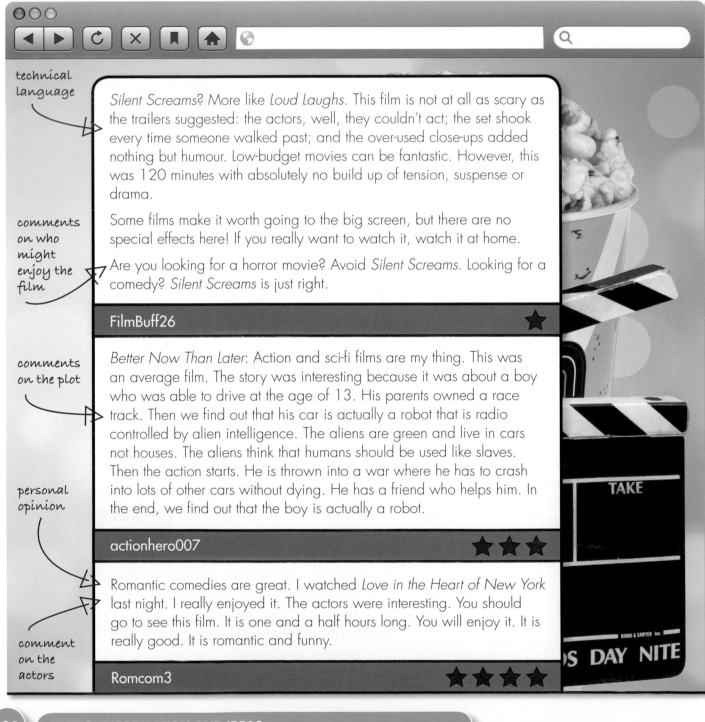

technical language

*Silent Screams*? More like *Loud Laughs*. This film is not at all as scary as the trailers suggested: the actors, well, they couldn't act; the set shook every time someone walked past; and the over-used close-ups added nothing but humour. Low-budget movies can be fantastic. However, this was 120 minutes with absolutely no build up of tension, suspense or drama.

Some films make it worth going to the big screen, but there are no special effects here! If you really want to watch it, watch it at home.

comments on who might enjoy the film

Are you looking for a horror movie? Avoid *Silent Screams*. Looking for a comedy? *Silent Screams* is just right.

FilmBuff26 ★

comments on the plot

*Better Now Than Later*: Action and sci-fi films are my thing. This was an average film. The story was interesting because it was about a boy who was able to drive at the age of 13. His parents owned a race track. Then we find out that his car is actually a robot that is radio controlled by alien intelligence. The aliens are green and live in cars not houses. The aliens think that humans should be used like slaves. Then the action starts. He is thrown into a war where he has to crash into lots of other cars without dying. He has a friend who helps him. In the end, we find out that the boy is actually a robot.

personal opinion

actionhero007 ★ ★ ★

Romantic comedies are great. I watched *Love in the Heart of New York* last night. I really enjoyed it. The actors were interesting. You should go to see this film. It is one and a half hours long. You will enjoy it. It is really good. It is romantic and funny.

comment on the actors

Romcom3 ★ ★ ★ ★

UNIT 3

## ACTIVITY 8

**a** In pairs, discuss which film review uses the most effective words, sentences and techniques to suit its **purpose**.

**b** Find a film review in a newspaper or magazine. How does the style and presentation of this review differ from the online user reviews on page 124? Consider length, language, tone, level of detail and the inclusion of layout features, such as images and sub-headings.

**c** What do you think the intended **audience** is for the review you have found? How is this suggested by the style and content?

## ACTIVITY 9

Write a review for a newspaper about a film you have watched. First, consider what the appropriate audience would be and then use a suitable tone, vocabulary and level of detail to engage your audience.

Your review could include:

- your overall opinion of the film and whether it met your expectations
- comments on the acting and actors
- brief details about the plot or how the film begins
- the special effects
- recommendations about who would enjoy the film
- a summary of your opinion at the end.

## FUNCTIONAL SKILLS TASK

**FUNCTIONAL SKILLS**

Look up a film, music or computer game website and read some of the online reviews. Take three or four reviews and compare the quality of each one. Look at:

- the language techniques used by each writer. How effective are they?
- how well the writer keeps to the task of reviewing (rather than just retelling the story)
- how effectively the writer conveys his or her opinion.

# TRY THIS!

## Being a teenager in the 21st century

The media often give negative images of teenagers. This is your chance to show what it really means to be a teenager in the 21st century and to challenge social stereotypes. The activity on the next page will require to you to combine information and entertainment to make 'infotainment'.

In this task you can practise writing different sorts of texts, using many of the techniques covered in this chapter.

Remember to:

- use lively language to entertain
- choose an appropriate tone for each piece of writing – will you be angry, humorous, serious, critical, chatty or formal?
- think about the layout of each piece of writing. How should an interview be set out on the page? What headings would work best? How can you use images to make the text look appealing?
- be as clear as possible so that other people will understand your point of view and the information you are sharing.

fashion

My view is...

## young sporting heroes

A great night out!

## ACTIVITY I

Create a two-page spread for a magazine on what it means to be a teenager in the 21$^{st}$ century.

You might want to include some of the following:

- headings, sub-headings and columns
- photographs and pictures showing what it is like to be a teenager
- a comment feature on something you feel strongly about. For example, the presentation of young people in the media or the legal rights of people your age.
- an interview with a celebrity
- an 'agony aunt' advice column
- an article on an event you took part in
- reviews of music/films/computer games.

**LEARNING CHECKLIST**

In this chapter you will learn to:

1 Understand texts, choosing parts that are relevant to certain ideas and comparing texts where necessary.

2 Interpret writers' ideas and viewpoints.

3 Explain how writers use language, style and form to create specific effects on the reader.

**AO3**

## Understanding viewpoints

People often have different viewpoints on the same situation. Some people's views may be shaped by personal feelings – we call this a 'subjective' viewpoint. For example, people who live close to a youth club might object to it because they dislike the noise. Other people may be in favour of a youth club because they believe that all young people should have a safe environment in which to meet friends. This is an 'objective' viewpoint, not linked to any personal reasons.

When discussing viewpoints, it is important to understand the key terms in the grid opposite:

| Key terms | Definition |
|---|---|
| perspective | the way that someone sees or thinks about something |
| bias | a viewpoint that is influenced by an underlying feeling for or against something; a biased account considers only one viewpoint |
| objective | not influenced by personal feelings or opinions |
| subjective | influenced by personal feelings or opinions |
| balanced argument | an argument that looks at all opinions and ideas before reaching a conclusion |

### ACTIVITY 1

Which key terms would you link with the following statements? (You can choose more than one key term per answer.)

a 'The children make too much noise. The park should close!'

b '88% of the people surveyed wanted to keep the park open.'

c 'I can see why parents want the park to stay open. However, it would be more useful to more people to have a supermarket there.'

### ACTIVITY 2

A local council has announced the closure of a park. Look at the list below and consider the perspective of each group of people. Identify whether they are likely to be for or against the park's closure and what their reasons would be.

- dog walkers
- a supermarket HQ looking to build a new premises
- parents of young children
- teenagers
- shoppers who want more local shops

# Letters to an MP

When presenting an argument to someone specific, a writer may choose to use a formal letter to add gravity to his or her point of view.

## FUNCTIONAL SKILLS TASK

Read the two letters below that have been written by local residents affected by the park closure.

- Who do you think will suffer most from the closure of the park? Use the information in the letters to back up your opinion.
- Your MP has a duty to represent the views of people who live in his or her area or 'constituency', regardless of the political party they belong to. Plan and draft a letter to your MP about a local issue that concerns you. Use the annotations on the letters to help you.

*FUNCTIONAL SKILLS*

16th July 2011

Dear Mr Graves MP,

*clear opening statement*

I am very concerned that a park in your constituency is about to be closed. The park is just 200 metres from my home. I go to the park every day. It is the only exercise I get.

*personal information*

However, it is not just for my sake that I write this letter. Many other retired people use the park as they see it as a welcoming and safe area to get some fresh air and gentle exercise. Many pensioners receive very little money. The park is free entertainment; a great break from sitting in the house. This is good for our mental wellbeing, physical health and overall comfort.

*introduces objective view*

*pattern of three to emphasize benefits*

Furthermore, young children, parents and teenagers also use the park. At least 150 people visit every day. A lot of your constituents will be upset if this open area is barred from them.

*statistic reinforces argument*

Finally, have you visited the park? It is the most beautiful space. There is a play area for toddlers and climbing frames for older children. Many teenagers play football on the open grass. It is welcome relief from the grey of the city.

*rhetorical question challenges the reader*

Yours sincerely,

Ben Amos

*emotive image*

---

Dear Mr Graves MP,

*subjective viewpoint*

*rhetorical questions convey urgent concern*

I am disappointed to hear that the council plans to close Greenfield Park. I am a local person who uses the park twice daily. I walk my dog and enjoy the fresh air. Where will I take my dog if the park is closed? In fact, where will all of the young children and teenagers go? You will have an unhappy group of constituents if you allow the closure. Please act now to save our park!

*direct plea is emotive*

*outlines future action*

I am willing to help by starting an online petition. I will also encourage other people to write to the council to show their displeasure. I enclose a picture of my dog, Rex. How could you deny this lovely dog his favourite activity twice a day?

*sentimental appeal*

Yours sincerely,

Gurpal Singh

## A different viewpoint

The extract below is from a supermarket website. The supermarket chain is thriving and looking to expand its business by buying new premises in towns and building new stores. It might well be interested in buying a town park that a council is selling off!

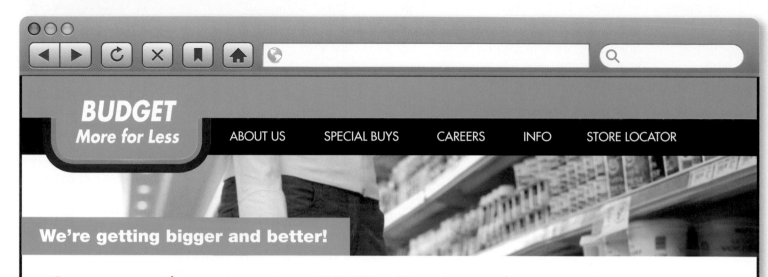

**BUDGET**
*More for Less*

ABOUT US     SPECIAL BUYS     CAREERS     INFO     STORE LOCATOR

### We're getting bigger and better!

Since opening our first store ten years ago, BUDGET has successfully established itself as one of the leading retailers in Europe.

We put our customers first, offering them unparalleled choice and quality of products at prices that everyone can afford.

Our success means that we are following an ambitious expansion programme, constantly seeking new employees, suppliers and premises.

**Make us an offer!**

Our investment programme means that we are looking for new sites, located in towns with a population of more than 8,000.

We are interested in:
- buying freehold sites that can be developed
- leasing existing space in retail parks.

Our promise to you…
- an efficient, business approach
- competitive pricing
- a generous commission package.

Get in touch now and together we can invest in a bright, affordable future for our customers.

---

### ACTIVITY 3

**a** What is the main purpose of this webpage?

**b** How does the writer use presentational devices to make his or her message effective? (Think about the layout, picture, links, headings, use of bullets, slogan, logo, rhetorical questions and imperatives.)

**c** If you were a director of Budget superstores, what might your viewpoint be on the sale of a park for development? Note down some arguments in favour of the purchase to present to your board. (Think about how it might benefit the local community as well as the company.)

## A campaign leaflet

Some people write campaign leaflets to make their views public and to persuade others to take joint action. Read the 'Shoppers Unite!' campaign leaflet below.

**SHOPPERS UNITE!**

Fed up with driving to the out-of-town supermarket?

Fed up with waiting for buses to go shopping?

**FACT:** The park is an eyesore. It is badly kept, full of litter and gives young people a site for vandalism and graffiti.

**FACT:** If the park were closed, a major supermarket would develop the site.

**THE ANSWER:**
Join our campaign to have more local shops.

Contact **shoppersunite@chadley.co.uk** for more information.

### ACTIVITY 4

People might respond to this leaflet in different ways.

**a** Explain how this leaflet may persuade some people to join Shoppers Unite.

**b** Explain how this leaflet may make other people more determined to keep the park!

### EXAMINER'S TIPS

- ✔ In your exam, aim to make a **range of points** rather than writing at length about one or two features. This will help you to show the examiner that you have fully understood the source texts and will keep your response fresh and interesting.

- ✔ When writing about presentational devices, ask yourself **why** the writer of the text chose to use them. How does this make the **written text** more effective?

### FUNCTIONAL SKILLS TASK

**FUNCTIONAL SKILLS**

In pairs or small groups, write your own campaign leaflet about an issue you feel strongly about. You need to:

- get your message across quickly and powerfully
- use repetition for effect
- be persuasive, using strong arguments
- make it clear what you want people to do.

# Reports

During the process of putting together a report, information is collected, interviews take place and surveys are carried out. All of this information is then collated and summarized under appropriate headings. Good reports will present this objectively and give a conclusion and recommendations at the end.

## Report on the Health of Students at Heartswell School

**Aim of this report**

This report aims to identify ways in which students at Heartswell School can be supported to improve their health.

**School meals**

Students are offered meals with a low salt, sugar and fat content. Every meal includes vegetables. However, only 60% of students eat school dinners. 26% of students eat packed lunches. 8% eat nothing and 6% are allowed out of school to eat. We have no data about what 32% of our students eat at lunchtime.

**Home meals**

Students completed a food diary about what they eat at home after school. 76% of students ate sweets or chocolate every day. 56% of students ate crisps or chips every day. In the survey, 38% of students stated that they ate five portions of fruit and vegetables every day.

**Physical Education department**

Physical Education is compulsory for all year groups for two hours per week. This should continue. However, on average, 11% of students do not take part in PE due to injury or illness.

**Out of school exercise**

In the survey, it was shown that 37% of students took part in team games such as football at least once a week. Another 23% of students take part in another form of exercise such as swimming or running.

**Smoking and drinking**

12% of students admitted to drinking alcohol at least once a week. Out of these students, the amount consumed averaged out as seven units per week. 8% of students admitted to smoking. This is slightly higher than the number of students caught smoking every week.

**Illness**

The school has a good attendance rate of 95%.

**Obesity**

According to the school nurse's records, 8% of students are overweight.

**Recommendations**

- Design and complete another survey to find out how to encourage more students to eat school dinners.
- Offer free fruit at break times.
- Explore the alternatives to eating chips, crisps, sweets and other unhealthy foods as part of PSHE lessons.
- Have regular free tasting sessions for the school dinners and ideas for alternative healthy snacks to eat at home.
- Start a Saturday sports club where students can play football and hockey.
- Target students known to smoke and drink with programmes showing how smoking and drinking can be dangerous to their health.

## ACTIVITY 5

**a** Is the report on page 132 written in an **objective** or **subjective** style? Give reasons for your answer.

**b** How does the report make use of facts and statistics, and what is the effect of these on the reader?

**c** What presentational features does the writer use and why?

## ACTIVITY 6

Copy and complete the grid below to show some different perspectives on and possible reactions to the report's recommendations.

| | PARENT | STUDENT | PE TEACHER | SCHOOL MEALS MANAGER | HEAD TEACHER |
|---|---|---|---|---|---|
| positive reactions to the report | It would be good to encourage students to eat more fruit. I like the sound of the free tastings. | | | | |
| negative reactions to the report | Packed lunches are cheaper than school dinners and I know they will eat them! | | | It will cost money to give free tastings. | |

## FUNCTIONAL SKILLS TASK

Do some Internet research regarding opinions on school dinners in the UK. Look at the manifesto Jamie Oliver posted on his website and then search for commentaries on other sites that oppose his arguments and viewpoints. How have the texts influenced your own opinion on the subject?

Consider
- the language used
- use of tone
- bias
- target audience.

FUNCTIONAL SKILLS

# Presenting a counter-argument

Below is a letter to the Head Teacher about the report on the health of students at Heartswell School.

Dear Mr Edwards,

We have met and discussed the report on the health of students. While we are happy that you have chosen to investigate this topic and plan to take action to improve health, we do have some concerns.

We are unhappy about the recommendations in the survey about home meals and packed lunches. After discussion, we have decided that students should not be encouraged to eat school dinners. We believe that students should be able to eat as they choose. This is a free country and secondary school students are old enough to make their own choices.

Furthermore, we are concerned that you are persistently insisting on two hours of Physical Education per week. In our brief survey, 70% of students stated that they disliked PE. Students are able to find their own exercise and sports outside of school.

Thank you for considering our opinion.

## ACTIVITY 7

**a** Who do you think this letter is from? Explain your answer with close reference to the text.

**b** How does the writer of the letter present a counter-argument to the recommendations given in the report on page 132?

**c** Do you agree with this viewpoint on the report? Explain your answer, with close reference to the text.

**d** Write a letter to the Head of Heartswell School from a different perspective.

## ACTIVITY 8

Imagine that another report has been written about raising students' attainment levels in their GCSE exams. It recommends that the school hours are extended to eight o'clock and that students should do a minimum of two hours private study at school every evening. Write a letter to the governors, presenting counter-arguments to these recommendations.

# Interpreting the writer's viewpoint

In your exam, one of the questions will test your ability to interpret the writer's viewpoint, ideas or attitude. The question may not use these actual words, but you will need to show the examiner that:

- you have a clear understanding of the writer's viewpoint or attitude
- you can back up your interpretation with references to the text.

The activities in this chapter focus on the skill of understanding different viewpoints. Below is a checklist of questions that you can ask yourself when interpreting the writer's viewpoint in your writing.

- What is the writer's attitude?
- What evidence can you find in the text to back this up?
- What tone does the writer use? (For example, is it humorous, serious or light-hearted?)
- What literary devices does the writer use and how effective are they?

## Trouble sleeping?

### MAKE YOUR BEDROOM A PLACE OF REST

Do you spend night after night lying awake, unable to drop off? Did you know that you are much more likely to have difficulty sleeping if your bedroom is filled with distractions?

How many electrical devices do you have in your bedroom? Do you have a TV, computer and a mobile? Anything else? Your bedroom should be a place of rest: somewhere to reflect, think and sleep. It should not be a place where you stay awake until the early hours watching TV or playing computer games. Unlike your TV, you need time to switch off. This means time to do nothing before you go to sleep.

Have you ever had a night's sleep interrupted by a mobile phone? Turn it off! Once your sleep is broken, it can be difficult to nod off again. Remember: the best form of sleep is sleep without distractions.

So - before you resort to counting sheep, make sure everything is switched off!

### OTHER THINGS YOU CAN DO
- Don't eat just before going to bed.
- Try to go to bed at the same time each night.
- Keep your room well ventilated.
- Avoid drinking tea and coffee after 6pm.

## ACTIVITY 9

With a partner, analyse the writer's viewpoint in the extract above. Use the checklist on this page to help you.

## EXAMINER'S TIPS

Always support your interpretations with close reference to the text. You do not need to include long quotations. Shorter ones embedded within sentences can be just as effective. Remember, however, wherever you use a quotation, you should always follow this up with an analysis of what it reveals.

# PREPARING FOR UNIT 3

## What will the questions be like?

This is the reading task; you will have an **hour** in the exam to complete the reading and write your responses. You will need to answer **two** questions.

- **Question 1** will focus on **reading for information**. This means that you will be asked to select relevant parts of the text and put these in your own words, without using quotations.

- **Question 2** will focus on **reading for interpretation**. This means that you will be asked to focus on how the material is presented and how it can be interpreted by the reader.

Each question will require a different type of response.

The questions on **reading for information** will ask you to select relevant parts of **what** is said and put them into your own words. The questions focused on **reading for interpretation** will expect you to analyse **how** things are said, so you need to concentrate on presentation, style and layout, rather than content.

## How should I divide my time in the exam?

Success in this unit depends on how carefully and thoroughly you read the unseen material. You should expect to spend up to 25% of the time reading and thinking about this before you start to write. Candidates who start writing immediately are less likely to gain high marks for their responses. The flow diagram on the next page shows possible one way to approach your reading.

### EXAMINER'S TIPS    OCR
RECOGNISING ACHIEVEMENT

- ✔ Either or both of the questions may be subdivided into more than one task. In the Foundation tier the questions will be more specific. In the Higher tier they will be more general.

- ✔ Check carefully which text each question refers to. The relevant title will be stated above the actual question.

- ✔ Note that in the Higher tier, Question 2 is worth more marks than Question 1, so you need to divide your time appropriately. In the Foundation tier, both questions carry the same marks, so you should divide your time equally between both.

Look carefully at the title and read briskly through right to the end. Some candidates lose marks because they stop reading before the end of the passage.

⬇

Skim through the whole text, scanning for any words that are unfamiliar, and if you can work out the meaning of them.

⬇

Re-read the conclusion and be sure of what it says.

⬇

Read through the passage again looking at how it is structured and how the paragraphs are linked.

⬇

Look again at the opening (the title and first paragraph) as an introduction.

⬇

Look at the task. It will be structured to help you frame your response. It may contain bullet-pointed headings to direct you to relevant material. Make sure you fully understand what is required.

⬇

Go back to the text and mark up the sections you need. Then begin your answer…

## EXAMINER'S TIPS

- ✔ Part of Question 1 is likely to ask you to 'use your own words'. This means you must avoid using quotations and instead write your own concise summary of what the writer is saying.

- ✔ For Question 2 you should look at the writer's language choices and say how they are effective in engaging the reader. You should use very brief quotations for this. The essential skills are analysis and evaluation.

- ✔ Make sure you give yourself (and stick to) strict time limits as you go through each part of the answer. You should expect to spend one hour on Section A, but you need to divide up that hour carefully.

**Source text 3.Ii**

## thepaper

# F1 boss ousted over driver ordered to crash

The head of Renault's Formula One team, London-based Italian multi-millionaire Flavio Briatore, was removed yesterday after claims that he ordered a racing driver to deliberately crash his car in a Grand Prix.

He allegedly asked the Brazilian Nelson Piquet Jr to crash at the race in Singapore last year. He then came unstuck in the most dramatic cheating scandal to hit Formula One after Piquet, a driver he sacked seven weeks ago, decided to spill the beans on his former boss to officials of motorsport's governing body.

Mr Briatore, 59, once dated the supermodels Naomi Campbell and Heidi Klum and now has a wife who is 30 years his junior, the Italian model Elisabetta Gregoraci, whom he married last year.

He is often seen enjoying the high life on his super-yacht, Force Blue.

Piquet explained how he had been asked to crash on purpose during lap 14 of the race. The aim of the subterfuge was to force the safety car off the track, which would benefit Piquet's team-mate, the Spanish driver Fernando Alonso, who went on to win the race.

To start with, Mr Briatore, a part owner of Queen's Park Rangers FC, denied all involvement, but yesterday he was sent packing. The F1A is taking the matter extremely seriously because Piquet was asked not only to throw the race deliberately but, in doing so, to put himself, other drivers, circuit marshals and spectators in danger.

Film of the crash shows Piquet's Renault coming out of a fast corner at about 120 mph, then going into a spin before smashing into the concrete walls on the other side of the track in an impact that crushed the right side of his car. The Brazilian was unhurt and no other drivers were injured.

Piquet said that he was asked 'to deliberately crash my car in order to positively influence the performance of the ING Renault Race team. I agreed to this proposal and caused my car to hit a wall and crash.'

# thepaper

OPINION

# The worst act of cheating in the history of sport

It is the worst single piece of cheating in the history of sport. We must accept that Renault, in refusing to defend its Formula One motor racing team against the allegation that one of its drivers was told to crash, is admitting that the allegations are indeed true.

That is to say that Nelson Piquet, a young man desperate to make his mark on the sport and yet struggling to keep up with its demands, was told to have an 'accident' at the Singapore Grand Prix.

Fernando Alonso was able to win a race he would otherwise have not, taking advantage of the safety procedures laid down in Formula One.

Renault – the company, not the Formula One team – has made its move. It has offered no defence to the charges and parted company with the team principal, Flavio Briatore. That is what happens when leading commercial concerns get mixed up in sport: their ultimate goal is profit, not sporting success. They are in it for image. They want to be associated with glamour and success, while the faintest hint of sordidness and cheating is an anathema.

This is no run-of-the-mill piece of skulduggery. The Renault team's crime was not merely fraudulent cheating; it was cheating as a potentially lethal act – as potential murder, if you like. This is not melodramatic. Deaths in motor racing still happen. They are not a relic of the wizard-prang days. Deaths come from crashes and no crash can be controlled.

Motor racing remains a very dangerous sport. It is supposed to be. Huge advances in safety measures have been made, but speed is by definition dangerous. It follows, then, that to play fast and loose in this sport is breathtakingly irresponsible.

# thepaper

## INSIDE TODAY
## Crashgate Scandal: What punishment lies in store for the shamed Renault team?

The first person at risk was Piquet, obviously. He was 23, eaten up with ambition, out of his depth, desperate to please. After him, every other driver in the race was put at risk by the decision to crash on purpose. And after that, the lives of marshals and spectators were wilfully risked – and for what?

A few points in a table. Money. Sporting prestige. Fame. Glory. It is this willingness to take risks with the lives of so many people that separates this event of cheating from the many others that have occurred with such regularity throughout the chequered history of sport.

This single incident is clearly different from long-term institutionalized cheating of which the East German drugs programme is the most notorious. When Ben Johnson took drugs to win the Olympic 100 metres in 1988, Johnson's life and health were at risk not those of his fellow competitors or track officials.

The so-called 'bloodgate' scandal in Rugby Union is just farce: a comic episode in which fake blood was used to attempt to gain a victory by fraudulent means. Even if Eduardo de Silva, the Arsenal forward accused of diving, had been found guilty, it would have been no more than a routine example of deception. The spear tackle on the Lions' rugby captain, Brian O'Driscoll, by Tana Umaga, the New Zealand captain, was a potentially crippling manoeuvre, but he was never charged, although some have suggested it was dangerous and premeditated as well as illegal.

But 'crashgate' is the worst…

*Simon Barnes*

## SECTION A: HIGHER TIER

**Sample task 3.1**

**Section A  Reading**

*You are advised to spend about one hour on Section A.*

*Read carefully the two passages 'F1 boss ousted over driver ordered to crash' and 'The worst act of cheating in the history of sport' and then answer Questions 1 and 2.*

**Question 1 Reading for Information**

*F1 boss ousted over driver ordered to crash*

Using the information in the passage, outline concisely:

- what you have learnt about Flavio Briatore

- the intentions and results of what Nelson Piquet did in the race.

Use your own words as far as possible.                          [14]

**Question 2 Reading for Interpretation**

*The worst act of cheating in the history of sport*

By referring to the presentation of the article and the language that he uses, explore the ways in which Simon Barnes conveys to the reader his views on how this incident relates to issues of cheating in sport.          [26]

## Student response 3.1 (Question 1)

Flavio Briatore is a very rich man who lives in London. He made racing driver Nelson Piquet smash his car up on purpose in the Singapore Grand Prix. Briatore, 59, has been out with well-known fashion models and has recently married a 29-year-old. He likes enjoying himself on his super-yacht. He is a part owner of Queen's Park Rangers Football Club.

He denied any responsibility for what happened and tried to divert attention away from himself and onto Piquet, but Renault sacked him as the team manager.

The intentions were to get Piquet to crash out of the race to try to get the safety car off the track so that Piquet's fellow Renault driver, Fernando Alonso, could win.

The results were that many lives, including Piquet's, were endangered. These included the lives of drivers, fans and track officials. Piquet's car spun and crashed into a solid wall at 120 mph. The right side of the car was crushed.

*neat summary: uses concise sentences*

*splits the two sections of the question effectively*

*well spotted: this point comes later in the article, but is relevant here*

*clear paragraph, packed with information*

## EXAMINER'S COMMENTS OCR

- A clear well-organized approach, showing complete understanding of the text and the task.
- This student has worded the response well, without copying directly from the text or using quotation.
- This is a high scoring response falling within the top band; more detail on Piquet in the race would make this response even stronger.

## Student response 3.1 (Question 2; extract)

**good analysis of presentational features, acts as an intro to writer's language choices**

The heading 'Opinion' makes it clear that this is one person's view and challenges us to disagree with it. A massive assertion about the incident follows, which again challenges the reader.

The picture is central with the text surrounding it: it is constantly in view as you read the text. The moment of impact it captures underlines the talk of potential results besides the actual ones. The 'inside today' box whets the reader's appetite.

Throughout the piece, the writer seeks to convince the reader that among many well-known sporting scams this is by far the worst. He emphasizes the facts and then evokes the potentially tragic consequences. Then he puts them in the context of the rest. Finally a triplet 'dangerous/premeditated/illegal': followed by cliché and bathos: 'crashgate is the worst' is the conclusion.

**clear overview of the structure, emphasizing the conclusion**

**skilfully identifies relevant language devices and their effect**

Colloquial and invented terms 'skulduggery' and 'wizard-prang' are used as contrasts to highlight the incident's seriousness. Adverbs 'breathtakingly' and 'wilfully' are intended to leave the reader doubt free; the use of lists conveys the awful possibilities: 'after him' and 'after that'.

Rhetorical questions such as 'for what?' challenge the reader to disagree and further one word sentences: 'Fame. Glory.' both stress the emptiness of success when compared with death. Finally, the use of 'chequered history of sport' links motor racing with the rest of the scams.

**well supported examples: an analysis of how the argument is developed**

## EXAMINER'S COMMENTS OCR

- The response is analytical and makes well-selected references to the text.
- There are some perceptive points about the presentation, although these points could be developed to show how these features reinforce the text.
- Overall, the response shows understanding and infers the writer's intentions; a top-band response.

**Source text 3.2i**

# Great Himalayan National Park

**Location**: 50 km from Kullu, Himachal Pradesh, India
**Area covered**: 754 sq km
**Major wildlife attractions**: Tragopan, Tahr, Snow Leopard
**Best time to visit**: April–May (The park remains open throughout the year)
**Places to stay**: Huts

| Info | Explore | About Us | Kids | Teachers |

## About the Great Himalayan National Park

The great Himalayas have always been a fascination for people around the world and the Great Himalayan National Park is no different. Situated in the Kullu district of Himachal Pradesh, the biodiversity of the park has made it a perfect habitat for some of the most exotic species of flora and fauna found anywhere in the world.

The park and the area around offer a plethora of options for tourists including bird-watching, religious pilgrimage and cultural tours. The park also has a tourist centre at Sai Ropa and an information centre at Larjee.

April and May are the best months to visit the park as during that time the snow melts and the conditions are ideal for walking and trekking. Winter is the only time when you stand an excellent chance of spotting rare animals like the Nilgiri Tahr and the Snow Leopard in the lower reaches of the park.

## Wildlife attractions in the Great Himalayan National Park

The park is home to more than 350 species of fauna including 31 mammals, 203 birds, three reptiles, nine amphibians and 127 insects.

If you hear a roar you may have come across a leopard or the highly-endangered and rarely seen Snow Leopard, even though these white creatures can't give a loud growl because of weak vocal tissues. Many smaller mammals can also be seen, including the Great Indian Flying Squirrel and the Indian Pika.

## Safaris

Most areas of the park have remained unexplored because of the sheer difficulty of the terrain, which lends the place a unique thrill and rawness that few other parks in the country can offer. Trekking in the park is no easy task and requires a person to be in shape. It is best to do some prior preparation in the form of deciding what to carry, and making a list of basic trekking equipment, such as tents and sleeping bags.

Source text 3.2ii

# Safari India

Info | Explore | About Us | Kids | Teachers

### A typical day on safari in India

If you are considering your first wildlife safari in India, here's a taste of what you can expect. We wake early and enter the park just as the sun is rising. Early morning and late afternoon are the best times to view wildlife as this is when the animals are most active.

There is an air of anticipation as we hope to see signs of overnight wildlife activity.

Your guide knows the area well and is an experienced wildlife tracker, but several pairs of eyes are always better than one, so you will probably want to join in, scanning the land for any movement or looking out for animal tracks.

When we are in forested areas, the undergrowth is often dense, so the guide will rely on the warning calls of other animals, such as monkey or deer. These cries are an exciting indication that something, possibly a tiger, is on the prowl through the undergrowth.

In India the jeeps stay on designated tracks to avoid damage to the environment and stress to the animals, but in several of the National Parks we use elephant to take us off the track and deep into the tigers' world. This does not bother the tigers but can give us the most wonderful sightings, perhaps of a tigress resting with her cubs or guarding the remains of an overnight kill. As well as tigers, you may see a

leopard, sloth, bear, jackal or wild boar, and many species of beautiful and amazing birds including India's national bird, the peacock. Depending on the areas you visit you may also see guar, swamp deer or Indian wild dogs; the photo opportunities are fantastic!

Mid-morning we get the chance to visit a local market or village, or just relax in the lodge grounds, before having lunch.

Late in the afternoon we head back into the park. The temperature is starting to drop and the animals that have been resting in the shade are beginning to stir. It is a good time to wait by a water hole or lake where we will often be lucky enough to see a succession of animals coming down to drink. It isn't unknown for a tiger to cool off by getting right into the water.

As dusk settles we head back to the lodge. It is time to reflect on the day's sightings and swap stories with other visitors.

It is, however, important to remember that although safari holidays are exciting and rewarding experiences, there is an element of unpredictability: no guarantees can be given with regard to which wildlife you will encounter or how often you will see any particular species. There are also access restrictions and rules to protect and minimize the impact of your presence on the animals and the environment.

## Sample task 3.2 (Question I)

### Section A Reading

*You are advised to spend about one hour on Section A.*

**Question 1 Reading for Information**

Read carefully the passage 'Great Himalayan National Park' and answer
Question 1a, 1b and 1c.

**1(a)** From **paragraph two** (beginning 'The park and the area…') write down
two attractions for tourists in the park.

Attraction 1 ...........................................................................................[1]

Attraction 2 ...........................................................................................[1]

**(b)** From **paragraph five** (beginning 'If you hear a roar…') identify two
phrases that describe the snow leopard and briefly explain their effect on
the reader.

Phrases about the snow leopard

1 ..........................................................................................................[1]

2 ..........................................................................................................[1]

Effects on the reader

1 ..........................................................................................................[1]

2 ..........................................................................................................[1]

**(c)** Re-read the passage from the beginning of **paragraph two**: 'The park and
the area…'

Using your own words as far as possible, outline the attractions of the park
and the nature of safaris around it. Do not use quotations in your answer.

................................................................................................................

................................................................................................................

................................................................................................................

................................................................................................................

........................................................................................................ [14]

## Sample task 3.2 (Question I)

Attraction 1 ...bird-watching.................................................................[1]

Attraction 2 ...wildlife viewing...........................................................[1]

**(b)** From **paragraph five** (beginning 'If you hear a roar…') identify two
phrases that describe the snow leopard and briefly explain their effect on
the reader.

Phrases about the snow leopard

1 ...highly endangered....................................................................[1]

2 ...rarely seen.............................................................................[1]

Effects on the reader

1 ...It makes me concerned for its survival.......................................[1]

2 ...It makes me want to go on safari to try to see it........................[1]

**(c)** Re-read the passage from the beginning of **paragraph two**: 'The park and
the area…'

Using your own words as far as possible, outline the attractions of the park
and the nature of safaris around it. Do not use quotations in your answer.

The park is set in the Himalayas, an area which people have always
found interesting. The most exciting plants and animals in the world
can be found there. Tourists have lots of things to do and can go on
cultural tours and religious pilgrimages. There is a tourist centre and
an information centre.

　　The best time to go is in the early summer because the snow has gone
and conditions are most suitable. But you only get to see the rare
animals like the snow leopard in the winter. There are lots of animals to
see, both big and small.

　　Safaris are difficult because of the landscape but they can be
exciting. You need to be fit to go on
them. You need to prepare and have
camping equipment with you. ..........[14]

### EXAMINER'S COMMENTS OCR

This student has answered both 1(a) and 1(b)
effectively, selecting appropriate information
from the source text. Answer 1(c) shows
understanding with some support from the text.
Overall, this falls into the upper band.

## Sample task 3.2 (Question 2)

### Question 2 Reading for Interpretation

Read carefully the passage 'Safari India'. Then answer Question 2a and 2b.

(a) How do the presentational features of this website add to its effect on the reader? [6]

(b) How does the website seek to engage its readers and persuade them to go on a safari in India?

In your answer you should write about:

- the attractive features of the safari
- the choice of words and phrases used to describe them. [14]

## Student response 3.2 (Question 2)

*neat summary point that sets up the rest of the answer*

The writing tries to make the reader feel that this will be an exciting but safe and responsible adventure. The word 'we' is repeated over and over again.

You can join the guide: 'several pairs of eyes are better than one' to 'scan' the land. They use elephants to go 'deep into the tigers' world'. Again this has a sort of a thrilling feeling to it. In the afternoon you may see a tiger cooling down in a water hole.

It's safe because you stay at night in the lodge, which isn't in the park itself. You can relax and chat to the other people there.

It's also responsible: it says using elephants 'doesn't bother the tigers' and that it doesn't make any promises about what you will or won't see. For example, it says 'we will often be lucky enough' and 'there is an element of unpredictability'.

I thought it did a good job of attracting the readers.

*understands effect on reader*

*good description, although more analysis would be better*

*shows effort to link directly with the language*

### EXAMINER'S COMMENTS OCR

There are some valid and well-made points here, but further development is needed to achieve a top-band mark.

# HOW TO APPROACH UNIT 3

## SECTION B: WRITING INFORMATION AND IDEAS

### What will I be assessed on?

In this section you will be marked according to Assessment Objective 4, which tests the skills listed below.

- **Write to communicate clearly, effectively and imaginatively, using and adapting forms and selecting vocabulary appropriate to task and purpose in ways that engage the reader.**
  You will be expected to develop your own ideas, and present these clearly using an engaging choice of vocabulary, tone and structure to keep your reader interested.

- **Organize information and ideas into structured and sequenced sentences, paragraphs and whole texts, using a variety of linguistic and structural features to support cohesion and overall coherence.**
  Careful planning before you start to write is essential in order to organize your work in a logical, accessible way.

- **Use a range of sentence structures for clarity, purpose and effect, with accurate punctuation and spelling.**
  Keeping your audience and purpose in mind will allow you to achieve the best effects with your language. Using different sentence structures can make your writing more engaging by varying the pace. Using short sentences and rhetorical questions can be used to create impact.

Your writing will be assessed on its quality as written communication. This means that your text needs to be legible and the **spelling**, **punctuation** and **grammar** accurate, so that the meaning is clear.

## EXAMINER'S TIPS

- ✔ Remember: the form of the writing and the audience it is for will both be specified in the task. So, check that you understand exactly what these are before you start planning.

- ✔ For this section, aim to spend up to 15 minutes planning, 40 minutes writing, and five minutes checking your work.

## LEARNING CHECKLIST

In this chapter you will learn to:

**1** Write clearly, with imagination, using suitable form and words to engage the reader.

**2** Write with a clear structure and sequence in sentences and paragraphs, using a variety of language features and techniques.

**3** Use a variety of sentence structures to create different effects, with correct punctuation and spelling.

**AO4**

## Using suitable form and words

Writing is a balancing act. When presented with a writing task you need to decide how formal it should be, what style, layout and tone to use and what sort of words and sentences are appropriate.

The scale below shows the choices that you have to make.

1 ⟵————————|————————⟶ 10

| Informal | Formal |
| Light-hearted | Serious |
| Opinionated | Factual |
| Emotive | impersonal |
| Subjective | Objective |

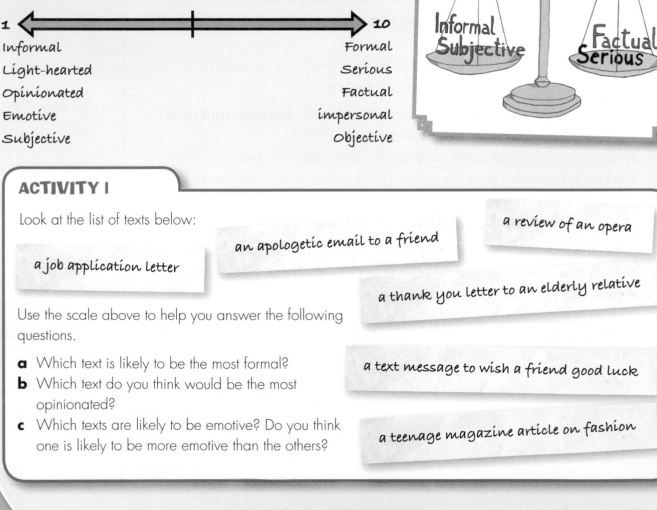

## ACTIVITY I

Look at the list of texts below:

a review of an opera

an apologetic email to a friend

a job application letter

a thank you letter to an elderly relative

Use the scale above to help you answer the following questions.

**a** Which text is likely to be the most formal?

**b** Which text do you think would be the most opinionated?

a text message to wish a friend good luck

**c** Which texts are likely to be emotive? Do you think one is likely to be more emotive than the others?

a teenage magazine article on fashion

UNIT 3

# Planning a piece of writing

Before completing a piece of writing you need to consider several things: its purpose, your audience, the layout, and the style. The mnemonic 'PALS' may help you to plan your work and to check it afterwards.

| TERM | EXPLANATION |
|------|-------------|
| P = Purpose | Why are you writing? Are you writing to entertain, persuade, report, explain, review or something else? |
| A = Audience | Who are you writing for? A friend, a boss, a teacher, an MP or someone else? |
| L = Layout | Should you write your text in paragraphs? Does it need subheadings or bullet points? Does it need a letter layout? |
| S = Style | What tone should your text be written in: lively, light-hearted, serious, thoughtful, angry? Should you use the first person (I), third person (he, she, it) or second person (you)? |

For example, if you are planning a review of a CD for a teenage magazine, you might note the following:

Purpose:    to review, inform and entertain
Audience:   teenagers
Layout:     some key information at the top, then paragraphs
Style:      light-hearted and lively; second person, 'You will enjoy this if you listen to…'

## ACTIVITY 2

**a** Plan an article for your local newspaper on a film festival at your school. At the festival, visitors, parents and students were invited to watch short films by students and vote on the best one. Use the mnemonic to help you plan.

**b** Write the newspaper article in full.

## EXAMINER'S TIPS

You may be asked to write a newspaper article in the exam so make yourself familiar with a range of different types of article, such as news stories, opinion pieces and reviews. You should also try to look at different types of newspaper, including tabloids, broadsheets and local papers.

# Different types of writing

Different types of writing generally use certain features or 'ingredients'. When you are set a writing task, you need to identify what type of writing is required, and what sort of features are usually included.

The panels below list examples of some of the main features and techniques used for different types of writing. Note that not all types of writing are included here and some texts will combine features from more than one type. For example, a travel guide may give factual information but also give a conclusion about an experience.

Remember also that one text type can be written in different styles. For example, a travel guide could be formal and factual, or more personal and entertaining. You need to adapt the language features and techniques depending on the purpose of your text and its audience.

## ACTIVITY 3

Match the following texts to their type (or types) below:

**a** a recipe

**b** a webpage comparing prices of mobile phones

**c** a magazine article about whether school students should be allowed to work from home on the Internet

**d** a piece of writing giving the writer's opinion of a film.

### Report

- headings and subheadings
- objective perspective
- formal language
- formal references to people, e.g. students, clients, colleagues etc.
- facts, figures and statistics
- clear and simple layout
- recommendations and/or conclusions at the end

### Writing to give instructions

- clear and factual style
- uses imperative verbs, e.g. get, put, cut, take etc.
- often uses subheadings
- impersonal tone (avoids using he, she, we or I)
- uses connectives, e.g. first, next, finally, before etc.

### Descriptive writing

- paragraphed
- should allow the reader to imagine the place, person or object described
- gives an overview as well as details
- adjectives
- adverbs
- similes
- appeals to the senses

### Review

- gives reasons why the product or experience is good or bad
- gives a conclusion
- often uses technical language or jargon
- gives an opinion, often subjective
- sometimes uses comparison

### Discursive writing

- balanced and objective
- gives arguments for and against a topic
- comes to a conclusion after considering the facts
- uses connectives, e.g. however, furthermore, moreover, similarly etc.
- often uses comparison

### Writing to entertain

- lively style
- informal, often humorous
- often uses 'you' to address the reader directly
- exaggeration
- familiar sayings
- slang words

## Structure: beginnings and endings

The beginning of a text is important as it sets the tone and style of your writing, and introduces the reader to the main content of your text. The ending of a text is important because it leaves the reader with a final impression of what you want to say. The ending might be used to summarize or emphasize the key points that you make in the main content of your text.

Below are some example beginnings and endings:

**1** C u l8tr m8!

**2** Have you ever thought of joining the most successful company in the UK?

**3** The best gadgets are friendly, fun and easy to use.

**4** I hope that you feel better soon.
We all miss you,
The Rangers Family

**5** Hi Steve, how are u gettin there 2nite?

**6** I know that you will support our campaign to help our most endangered animals.
Yours sincerely, Emily Hanover

### ACTIVITY 4

**a** With a partner, discuss what types of text the extracts above might come from and the impression they have on the reader. (For example, 4 is from a personal letter, which aims to make the reader feel valued.)

**b** Write a beginning and ending for each of the following tasks:
- a letter to a friend who has moved to another country
- a magazine article looking at the effects of binge drinking
- an email to a company asking them to donate products for a charity auction.

**c** Compare your beginning and ending for each text with a partner. Which are the best sentences? Why?

### FUNCTIONAL SKILLS TASK

**FUNCTIONAL SKILLS**

A friend is writing a letter to the council about noisy neighbours. Look at the way he has started and ended. What advice would you give him about letter writing?

> Mr Patel,
>
> I am furious! When are you going to do something? You lot are useless!
> [...]
> Never mind sorting out the rubbish, drains and roads! Kick out my neighbours!
>
> Yours angrily,
>
> A Friend

# Language techniques: tone

To create a successful piece of writing you need to carefully consider your **tone**. The following words describe different tones:

light-hearted

assertive    cold

angry    calm    reflective

fearful    tense    sympathetic

lively    firm    romantic

enthusiastic    humorous    serious

business-like    brisk or efficient

thoughtful    frustrated    friendly

## ACTIVITY 5

**a** Identify the tone (or tones) used in each of the extracts on the right.

**b** Write the first paragraph for an article on smoking for a teenage magazine.

- First, write it in a serious, formal tone for people worried about their health.
- Next, write it in a lively way to engage (interest) young people and encourage them to think about the dangers of smoking.
- What did you have to change?

**1** Walk to town? She must be mad. It's miles away! It would take us all night to get there!

**2** The ball was midair when Trouth nudged it to the right, out of Carlton's reach.

**3** The hospital must close. The level of care it offers patients is not consistent or reliable.

**4** We can all do our bit to help save the planet: walking rather than driving; switching off lights; turning down the heating. None of this requires too much effort does it?

## FUNCTIONAL SKILLS TASK

FUNCTIONAL SKILLS

Plan and write a letter to a real person for a real purpose using an appropriate tone. For example, write a letter of complaint to a cinema (about the noise, price or length of the queues) or a letter to a relative to persuade them to let you come and stay. You may wish to use more than one tone for added impact. Ask a partner to comment on how effective your use of tone is in your writing (i.e. is it likely to achieve the result you want?).

UNIT 3

## Choosing the style of your writing

Many texts, such as magazine articles, combine a range of language and structural features with a consistent use of tone to give them a particular **style**. Before you write your response to this task in the exam, you need to plan the style of your work, thinking carefully about the topic and your target audience.

Below are some extracts from magazine articles, showing headlines and first lines.

1. **HEALTH: Mobile Phones** — Scientists fear that mobiles could damage your health.
2. **footballers foul and fall** — Should footballers be role models?
3. **Riot at the Oscars** — A riot of colours and styles this year.
4. **Pet Show Stars** — A beagle bursts into rhythmic barks to the theme tune of *Animal Zoo*.
5. **LITTER LOUTS** — Smith investigates how you feel about the idea of fines for people who drop litter.
6. **Top Ten Days in the UK** — Looking for something to do this weekend?

### ACTIVITY 6

**a** With a partner, discuss the possible **purpose** of each article above.

**b** What **tone** of language would you expect the writer to use in each article?

**c** What other language features would you expect to find in each?

### ACTIVITY 7

Choose one of the headlines above and plan and write the whole magazine article.

Plan the **structure** of your article carefully. For example, for 'Health: Mobile Phones' you could divide paragraphs into reasons for and against using mobile phones, plus a conclusion stating how to reduce any health risks.

### EXTENSION TASK

Write a magazine article as 'infotainment' (a mix of information and entertainment). The article is for older people (65+) explaining current trends in modern music. Your challenge is to write in the style most appropriate for this type of audience.

### EXAMINER'S TIPS

**OCR**
RECOGNISING ACHIEVEMENT

It is important to establish exactly what audience you are writing for so that your piece of writing will be appropriate in terms of vocabulary, tone and structure. Putting careful thought into this will help you gain marks in the exam.

## Style and audience

Read the two recipes below. Note that each one is written in a different style to appeal to a different audience. The annotations indicate features that affect the style of the texts.

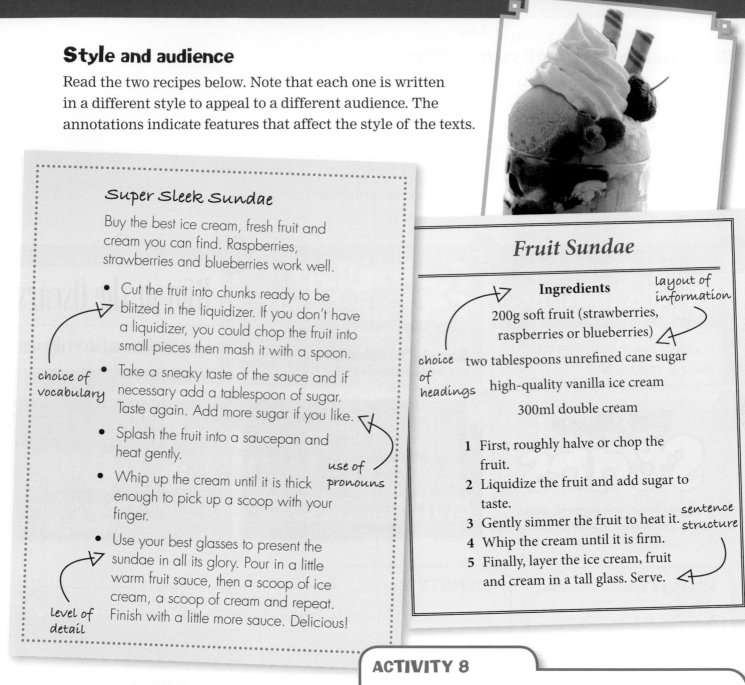

### Super Sleek Sundae

Buy the best ice cream, fresh fruit and cream you can find. Raspberries, strawberries and blueberries work well.

- Cut the fruit into chunks ready to be blitzed in the liquidizer. If you don't have a liquidizer, you could chop the fruit into small pieces then mash it with a spoon.

*choice of vocabulary*

- Take a sneaky taste of the sauce and if necessary add a tablespoon of sugar. Taste again. Add more sugar if you like.

- Splash the fruit into a saucepan and heat gently.

*use of pronouns*

- Whip up the cream until it is thick enough to pick up a scoop with your finger.

- Use your best glasses to present the sundae in all its glory. Pour in a little warm fruit sauce, then a scoop of ice cream, a scoop of cream and repeat. Finish with a little more sauce. Delicious!

*level of detail*

### Fruit Sundae

**Ingredients**

*layout of information*

200g soft fruit (strawberries, raspberries or blueberries)

*choice of headings*

two tablespoons unrefined cane sugar

high-quality vanilla ice cream

300ml double cream

1. First, roughly halve or chop the fruit.
2. Liquidize the fruit and add sugar to taste.
3. Gently simmer the fruit to heat it.

*sentence structure*

4. Whip the cream until it is firm.
5. Finally, layer the ice cream, fruit and cream in a tall glass. Serve.

## FUNCTIONAL SKILLS TASK

Choose a recipe from a book or the Internet. Identify the audience it is aimed at. Consider the vocabulary, tone and level of detail used. Adapt the tone and style of the recipe to suit a different audience, for example, children or people who don't enjoy cooking.

## ACTIVITY 8

**a** Describe the **tone** in each recipe. Which is the most informal? Pick out words from the text to support your answer.

**b** Which text uses the greatest variety of sentence types? What effect does this have? (Look in particular at the end of each recipe.)

**c** Which style of recipe do you prefer? Why?

### EXTENSION TASK

The recipe format is sometimes used to give humorous advice. Write a recipe for getting a date or planning a holiday. Provide a list of 'ingredients' and use a step-by-step 'method' to structure the main text.

## Practise planning and writing

This chapter has covered the factors that you need to take into account when planning a piece of writing. The diagram below suggests one way of drawing this together into a single approach to the task. Use the diagram to help you complete the activities that follow.

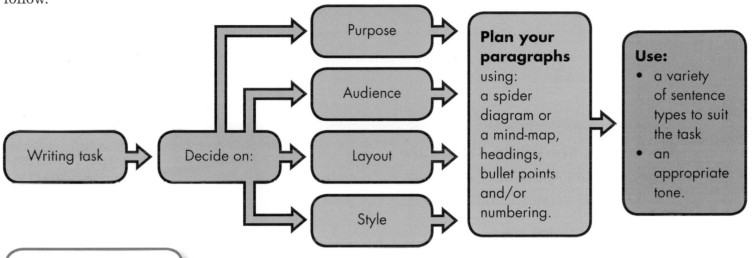

### ACTIVITY 9

Plan three different texts. Copy and complete the grid below in as much detail as possible.

| TASK | 1. MAGAZINE ARTICLE ON THE DANGERS OF SUNBATHING | 2. NEWSPAPER OPINION PIECE ON HOSPITAL FOOD | 3. REVIEW OF TWO DIFFERENT FILMS FOR A WEBSITE FOR TEENAGERS |
|---|---|---|---|
| Purpose | | | |
| Audience | | | |
| Layout | | | |
| Style | | | |

### ACTIVITY 10

Plan and write an article for your local newspaper persuading families to look after a rescue animal.

## LEARNING CHECKLIST

In this chapter you will learn to:

1 Write clearly, with imagination, using suitable form and words to engage the reader.

2 Write with a clear structure and sequence in sentences and paragraphs, using a variety of language features and techniques.

3 Use a variety of sentence structures to create different effects, with correct punctuation and spelling.

AO4

## Variety in sentence structure

To create an interesting piece of writing, you need to make your sentences varied, using different sentence structures. For example:

- a **simple sentence**, with one clause and one verb, can be used to create impact or make a strong statement.

- a **compound sentence**, with two main clauses linked with a connective such as 'and', 'but' or 'or', can be used to link together ideas, or to build a description.

- a **complex sentence**, consisting of a main clause that can stand on its own and a subordinate clause, can be used to pack more information into your writing.

Using a range of punctuation can also add variety to your sentence types; for example, using question marks and exclamation marks or using a semi-colon to separate clauses and phrases on a similar topic.

Exams! Who needs them? I can live without them. However, qualifications are important if you want to do further education, or if you want to find a job. But there always seems to be more interesting things to do than schoolwork, even if it's just tidying my room!

## ACTIVITY I

**a** Read the speech bubble on the right. Identify as many different sentence structures and types as you can.

**b** Write your own short paragraph, on the subject of homework, or another topic of your choice. Use a mix of sentence structures and types to make your writing varied and interesting for the reader.

UNIT 3

# Connectives

Connectives act like glue – they fix ideas together in sentences and connect sentences together in paragraphs. Without them a text can seem fragmented; lots of random ideas without a logical flow between them.

Connectives can act as co-ordinators in compound sentences, linking together separate clauses. For example:

> We went shopping <u>and</u> met the others for a pizza.

Alternatively, connectives can be used to create the link between a main clause and a subordinate clause. For example:

> <u>Even though</u> I'd rather go to the football match, I have agreed to visit my grandmother on Saturday afternoon

Connectives can do different jobs. They can indicate place, time or allow the writer to give a reason for something. They can help to organize information by adding, sequencing, comparing, contrasting and qualifying.

## ACTIVITY 2

Choose three connectives from the list below and write three example sentences to show their use:

- as a co-ordinator
- in forming a complex sentence (with a subordinate clause)
- as a cohesive marker (showing time, place or sequence).

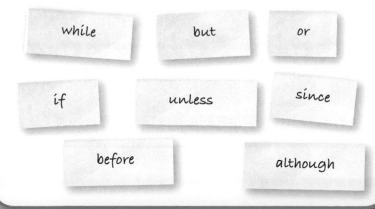

while    but    or

if    unless    since

before    although

## ACTIVITY 3

Play 'pass the connective'! This game is a competition for two teams to test their skills with connectives.

1  Choose a topic, such as 'how to enjoy the holidays'.
2  A player from Team A gives a player from Team B a connective.
3  The Team B player has to come up with a sentence on the topic, using the given connective. If they succeed, they score a point for their team.
4  The Team B player then gives a Team A player another connective.
5  Play continues, with a time limit of 10 seconds to come up with a sentence. Reduce the time limit to increase the pace!
6  The team with the most points at the end of the game wins. (Ensure that equal turns have been taken on each side.)

## Sorting out paragraphs

Your writing will have more logic and style if you think about how ideas are grouped together into paragraphs. Here are some of the main topics that can be the focus of paragraphs, or the reason to begin another one:

- introduction or conclusion
- place
- time
- direct speech
- new person/event
- change of topic.

### ACTIVITY 4

**a** Look carefully at the extract from a website printed below, and decide the purpose of each paragraph.

**b** How does each paragraph draw the reader in?

**c** Look at the third paragraph. Explain how the writer combines objective and subjective statements. What is the effect of opening with a fact?

**d** What is the impact of concluding paragraph 3 and paragraph 4 with a short sentence?

# DERWENT VALLEY MILLS

## Info

In December 2001, the Derwent Valley Mills in Derbyshire became a World Heritage Site. This international designation confirms the importance of the area as the birthplace of the factory system.

Here in the 18th century, water power was successfully harnessed for textile production. This brought hundreds of workers together in one place and changed employment in the valley from agriculture to industry in the first 'modern' factories.

The Derwent Valley Site stretches for 15 miles from Matlock Bath to Derby. It contains a fascinating series of historic mills and workers' cottages and is ideally placed for a holiday base. Why not pay a visit?

Regular guided tours are given by local volunteers who possess a wealth of knowledge on the area's history. Click here for details.

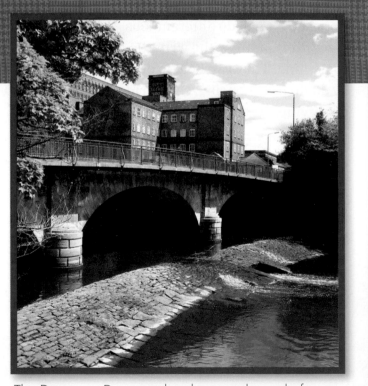

The Discovery Days weekend runs at the end of October, with walks, talks and children's activities: click here to find out more about this year's events.

## Letters and reports

The form and structure of informal letters, emails and text messages can be quite straightforward. The form and structure of formal letters and reports, however, is often more complicated. Use this chart to remind yourself of some key features:

| IS IT A LETTER? | IS IT A REPORT? |
| --- | --- |
| Include your address and date on the right-hand side. | Use a title which states the subject briefly. Who is it for? |
| Put the name and address of the person you are writing to on the left-hand side. | First paragraph outlines topic. |
| Know the name? 'Dear Mr Smith,' ends with 'Yours sincerely,' and a signature. | Later paragraphs explore points fully. |
| State the subject clearly in the first paragraph then continue. | Final paragraph gives recommendations. |
| No name? 'Dear Sir/Madam,' ends with 'Yours faithfully,' and a signature. | |

### FUNCTIONAL SKILLS TASK

**a** In pairs, discuss the format needed for the following tasks and plan how you might structure them:
  - a report on the benefits of owning a pet
  - a letter to the editor of your local paper about the dangerous state of a park playground
  - a report to the council about improving youth facilities in your area.
**b** Choose one of the tasks and write it in full.
**c** Swap the first draft of your text with another pair. Proofread each other's work, checking spellings and punctuation. Feed back on what could be improved.

### EXAMINER'S TIPS

OCR
RECOGNISING ACHIEVEMENT

When you are writing a formal letter, you need to use formal language. This includes using **Standard English** and avoiding slang or colloquialisms. A formal writing style is impersonal, polite, clear and to the point.

## Webpages and leaflets

We get a great deal of useful information from websites and leaflets – anything from world news to ticket prices for music gigs. Both webpages and leaflets use visual clues to guide their readers, and recognizing these layout features is part of being able to 'read' such texts. Look at some examples of these features below:

captions

headings and sub-headings

video clips

lists/tables

inset boxes with key facts

bullet points

hyperlinks to other parts of the site

question and answer sections

photos, maps and diagrams

different fonts, use of bold and italics, underlining

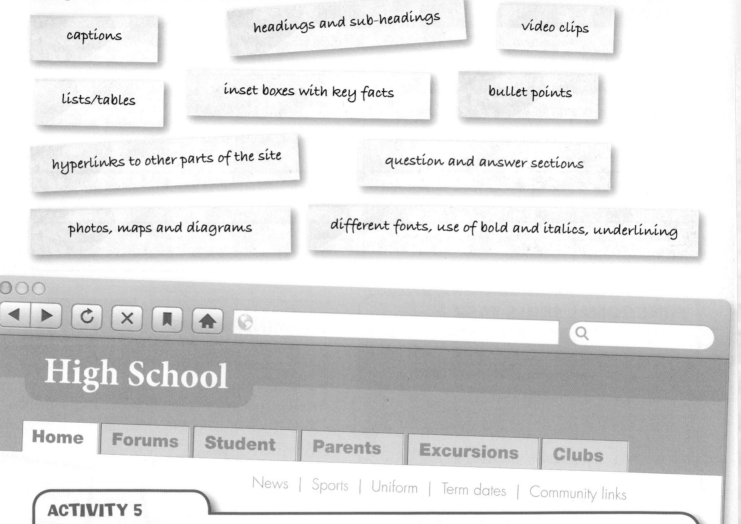

# High School

| Home | Forums | Student | Parents | Excursions | Clubs |

News | Sports | Uniform | Term dates | Community links

### ACTIVITY 5

Look at your school's website and see how many of the features listed above appear. How successfully are they used? Who is each feature intended to appeal to: parents or students or both? Now compare what you have found with websites for other schools in your local area. Make notes and report back to the whole class.

### EXTENSION TASK

Write a critical review of your school's website for your Head Teacher, identifying strengths and weaknesses, and any changes you would recommend. You may wish to divide up your report into sections, examining different aspects of the website; for example, accuracy of text, amount of information, how up-to-date it is, how easy it is to navigate around and use of visuals.

## Newspaper reports

Newspaper reports should always aim to answer the following: **what** happened, **where** and **when** it happened, **who** was involved, and if possible, **how** and **why** it happened.

Along with headlines and subheadings, newspaper reports frequently feature a standfirst paragraph, quotations and emotive language. The standfirst paragraph is used to summarize the key points of the story.

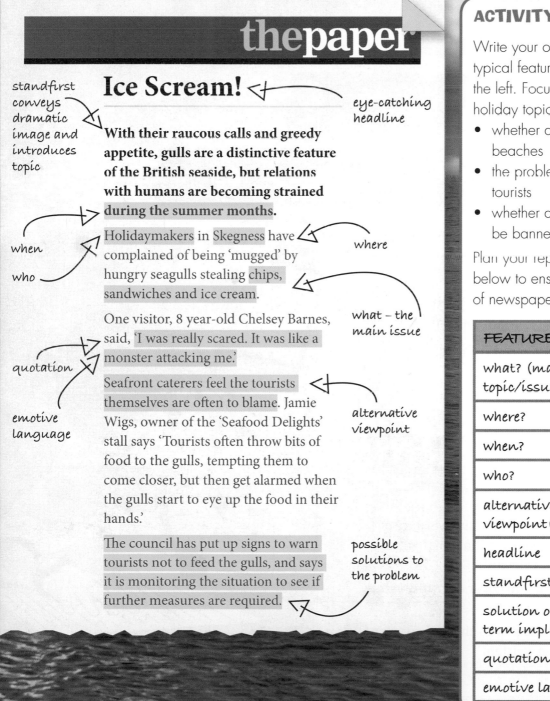

**thepaper**

### Ice Scream!

**With their raucous calls and greedy appetite, gulls are a distinctive feature of the British seaside, but relations with humans are becoming strained during the summer months.**

Holidaymakers in Skegness have complained of being 'mugged' by hungry seagulls stealing chips, sandwiches and ice cream.

One visitor, 8 year-old Chelsey Barnes, said, 'I was really scared. It was like a monster attacking me.'

Seafront caterers feel the tourists themselves are often to blame. Jamie Wigs, owner of the 'Seafood Delights' stall says 'Tourists often throw bits of food to the gulls, tempting them to come closer, but then get alarmed when the gulls start to eye up the food in their hands.'

The council has put up signs to warn tourists not to feed the gulls, and says it is monitoring the situation to see if further measures are required.

Annotations:
- standfirst conveys dramatic image and introduces topic
- eye-catching headline
- when
- who
- where
- what – the main issue
- quotation
- emotive language
- alternative viewpoint
- possible solutions to the problem

### ACTIVITY 6

Write your own newspaper report, using typical features as shown in the article on the left. Focus on another controversial holiday topic, such as:

- whether dogs should be allowed on beaches
- the problem of litter dropped by tourists
- whether amusement arcades should be banned from the seafront.

Plan your report first, using the grid below to ensure you include key features of newspaper reports.

| FEATURE | EXAMPLE |
|---|---|
| what? (main topic/issue) | |
| where? | |
| when? | |
| who? | |
| alternative viewpoint(s) | |
| headline | |
| standfirst | |
| solution or long-term implications | |
| quotations | |
| emotive language | |

## Consolidating your writing skills

Before you tackle any writing activity, there are questions you need to ask yourself. The 'PALS' mnemonic is useful to bear in mind at this planning stage:

**P**urpose: why are you writing?

**A**udience: who are you writing for?

**L**ayout: how should the text be structured and presented?

**S**tyle: what tone should it be written in? What vocabulary would be appropriate?

While you are writing, check the following points.
- Am I using appropriate sentence lengths and styles?
- Am I using effective punctuation?
- Am I using interesting, varied vocabulary?

When you have finished writing, check:
- Is my spelling correct?
- Have I used punctuation accurately?

Should I put a comma here?

### EXAMINER'S TIPS

**OCR** RECOGNISING ACHIEVEMENT

Remember to:
- ✔ frequently refer back to the wording of the task, to make sure that what you are writing is still relevant to it!
- ✔ make sure that you cover everything that you are asked to cover
- ✔ allow time at the end to check through what you have written.

UNIT 3

Choose one of the writing tasks in the activity below. Use the advice given on page 164 to produce an interesting text that will engage your reader.

## ACTIVITY 7

a Write a feature article for your school newspaper complaining about coverage of music on television.

b A large dog has been wandering loose in your town and has been seen near a school and a children's playground. No one has been attacked yet, but people are afraid. Write a newspaper report to appear in the local evening paper.

## EXTENSION TASK

Write a report on a controversial subject you feel strongly about. This can be used as the basis for a speech to the class, or a leaflet to go on display in the school library.

Suggested topics:

- young people and alcohol
- animal welfare in modern farms
- the impact of reality TV on viewers
- the problem of knife crime and youth violence.

## FUNCTIONAL SKILLS TASK

**FUNCTIONAL SKILLS**

You work for an environmental awareness group, and are leading a campaign to promote a more 'green' way of living. Create a series of webpages to inform the general public about ways they can make their lifestyles more eco-friendly. Consider which style, tone, language and layout features will be most effective.

# PREPARING FOR UNIT 3

## SECTION B: WRITING INFORMATION AND IDEAS

## What will the task require me to do?

In this section you will need to produce **one** continuous written response from a choice of two tasks. You have **one hour** to complete this task and it is worth **40 marks**.

Although you might be tempted to do this task first in the exam it isn't a very good strategy. The writing tasks often build on what you have read in Section A, so it is far better to focus on this section last.

The task will advise you on what form your piece of writing should take, who it should appeal to and what the function of it should be. You should read the task wording carefully before planning your response.
A breakdown of the task structure is given below:

**Background**: the task will give a context for the piece of writing, e.g. who you are and why you are writing.

⬇

**Main task**: This explains what you need to write, in what form, e.g. a letter or a newspaper article.

⬇

**Prompts**: These will contain bullet points, which will give you an idea of what aspects to cover and some possible starting sentences.

## EXAMINER'S TIPS

- ✔ Read the whole question thoroughly, at least twice, taking note of exactly what you are being asked to do. Do not start writing until you are absolutely sure of what is required of you.

- ✔ Think carefully about who your audience is and make sure your style and vocabulary are suitable.

- ✔ Remember that you are giving information that needs to be clear, fluent and accessible.

- ✔ Avoid slang and jargon unless they are particularly appropriate for the task and audience.

## How can I do my best in the exam?

Success in this writing task will depend on how methodically you approach it in the exam. It's useful to have established and practised a 'drill' that you know works for you when dealing with this type of writing task. It should ensure that you write relevantly and concisely, and that you make the most of the time available.

You and your teacher will discuss and refine what works best for you, but below is one possible drill.

Make sure you understand the audience you are writing for and the form that the writing is to take.

Decide how much you are going to write (by the time you take the exam you will have enough experience to know what you can manage in an hour). Expect to use all the time available in the exam working. Finishing early will not gain you any extra marks!

Then plan the paragraphs/topics and the way they link both to the conclusion and to each other. A good plan means that you have a skeleton before you start writing. Then, as you write, you can 'flesh out' that skeleton and concentrate on the mechanics of your writing: the spelling, punctuation, grammar and general legibility.

Plan your work, starting with the subject matter and going on to the conclusion you will reach. This is like going to a railway station and buying a ticket for your chosen destination rather than simply getting on the train and wondering where you might end up!

Finally, make sure that your opening engages and involves the reader.

# SAMPLE TASKS

## SECTION B: HIGHER TIER

### Sample task 3.3

**Section B Writing**

*You are advised to spend about one hour on Section B.*

*Answer one question.*

*This answer will be marked for writing. Plan the answer and write it carefully. Leave enough time to check through what you have written.*

**Question 3**

**Either**

**(a)** The Head of your school/college has asked you to speak informally to new students giving them some ideas on how to be successful.

**Write the words of your talk.**

You should include:

* dos and don'ts based on the experiences of you and your friends

* a selection of school/college scenarios: lessons, games, extra activities, etc. [40]

**Or**

**(b)** Heroic Failures. A local newspaper is running a competition for people to write about their real or imagined experience of something that started out as a good cause but ended in failure.

**Write the article.**

The editor has suggested that you could use one of the following opening lines. You can, of course, start off exactly as you wish.

* 'I knew it wouldn't work in the first place but…'

* 'It seemed a really good idea at the time…'

* 'There was no way we could possibly have known that…' [40]

## Student response 3.3 (Question 3a)

Hi guys, now listen up!

The best thing about this place is that it gives you a second chance when you mess up. And we all mess up sometimes. The thing to do then is learn to get it right next time and be successful.

When I was in Year 8 I thought I'd done all the work I needed in Year 7 and switched off. Or, rather, switched on: to my iPod 24/7. Luckily for me, my teachers got me back on track. Now I'm looking forward to good GCSEs and a place in the sixth form.

The friends you make in the first weeks of term will probably be the ones you stick with for the next five years or more, so choose them carefully. Don't put on an act: people will see through it and it'll take twice as long to get a decent group of mates. Have the confidence to be yourself and others will respect you.

DO join in things. If you like sports there's football, netball, cricket and rounders going on every break and lunchtime and you can trial for the school teams if you want. If sport isn't your thing there are all sorts of musical and drama things to do. If there isn't a club on offer that suits your interests you could even set up one up of your own. My friends and I decided to set up a band in Year 9, which now has quite a fan base! We spoke to our Head of Year and she arranged for us to use the Assembly hall on Wednesdays to practise.

In lessons, make sure you DO listen to the teachers. The teachers here all have outstanding abilities when it comes to detecting whether or not you are listening. You can be sure that the second you drop off is the second you will be called upon to answer a qustion!

**Margin annotations:**

adopts an apt tone and engages the target audience

develops the point made in previous paragraph, including personal experience

makes a very important point at the outset

a serious point using more suitably 'serious' language

lightens the tone with less serious subject matter

follows the first bullet point in the instructions for the task

**Student response 3.3 (Question 3a)**

effective sentence structure helps to add weight to this point

When the time comes to make your subject choices, think wisely. Don't just pick the subjects that your best friend wants to do. You probably won't get good GCSEs if you make decisions for the wrong reasons.

And DON'T get on the wrong side of the staff; they're here to help you. But they won't if you're rude to them and don't do what they say.

I've had a great time here. Take a moment to think about what I've said and you will too. Good luck!

a clear and positive conclusion

## EXAMINER'S COMMENTS OCR
RECOGNISING ACHIEVEMENT

- A confident answer, although a little brief. It sticks to the informal talk format throughout which is appropriate to the task and purpose.
- The ideas are developed in a clear sequence but these could have included more detail in places.
- The spelling, grammar and punctuation are accurate.
- This is an upper- to top-band response.

## SECTION B: FOUNDATION TIER

### Sample task 3.4

**Section B Writing**

*You are advised to spend about one hour on Section B.*

**Question 3**

> *Answer one question.*
> *This answer will be marked for writing. Plan your answer and write it carefully. Leave enough time to check through what you have written.*

**Either**

**(a)** Write a letter to friends/family members who are going to visit a place you know well for the first time.

**Write your letter.**

Keep their personalities, likes and dislikes in mind and say:

- which aspects of the place they should go to and why
- which aspects of the place they would better avoid and why.

These DO NOT have to be in equal measure. [40]

**Or**

**(b)** The editor of your school/college magazine has asked you to write an account of your ideal holiday.

**Write your article.**

Remember to:

- give as much detailed information as you can
- say why it is your first choice. [40]

uses the correct form of address and explains the reasons for the letter

Dear Aunt Sophie,

Thanks for letting us know you're going to emigrate to Sydney later in the year. I didn't know whether you are on the Internet and whether I could send an email, so I'm writing a letter instead. Not something I do very often these days!

Australia is great, it's such a cool place to live. Mum and Dad haven't had any regrets since we came over here and neither have I. The best thing about it is the weather: we do get winter but it's much warmer than in the UK. Summer seems to last much longer: there are lots of good swimming days.

shows good awareness of interests of her reader

Seriously, though, you need to look very carefully at where you're going to live. The places that look the best near the city and on the coast are way more expensive than the more remote areas that are a bus or train ride away from the centre. The city can be noisy and quite scary at night. As you come from a small village in England, I think you should look for the same sort of place over here. I hope you're going to live somewhere near us.

a longer paragraph to make a more serious point: sentence structure is secure

There are loads of things you'll love seeing in Oz. My favourite (which we're already planning to take you to) is the Great Barrier Reef. You can go out in a boat with a glass bottom and look at all the different fish and coral stones. Mum said you've taken up playing tennis. Well, sport is really big out

**Student response 3.4 (Question 3a) continued**

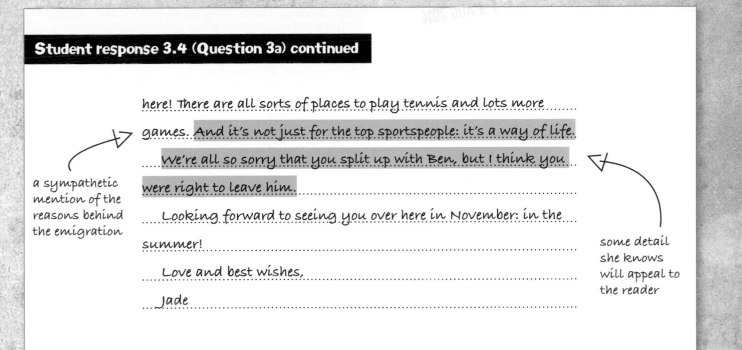

here! There are all sorts of places to play tennis and lots more games. And it's not just for the top sportspeople: it's a way of life.

We're all so sorry that you split up with Ben, but I think you were right to leave him.

Looking forward to seeing you over here in November: in the summer!

Love and best wishes,

Jade

a sympathetic mention of the reasons behind the emigration

some detail she knows will appeal to the reader

### EXAMINER'S COMMENTS OCR RECOGNISING ACHIEVEMENT

- The answer focuses on the task throughout and the letter format is used convincingly.

- There is evidence of a clear sense of audience.

- There text is structured well and the writer effectively develops and links each point to the next. The ending is well thought-out.

- The text is not ambitious, but it is clear and accurate; a middle- to upper-band response.

# OXFORD
## UNIVERSITY PRESS

*£18.99  O67939*
*Gravesend  428*
*1 9 AUG 2014*

Great Clarendon Street, Oxford OX2 6DP

Oxford University Press is a department of the University of Oxford.
It furthers the University's objective of excellence in research,
scholarship, and education by publishing worldwide in

Oxford   New York

Auckland   Cape Town   Dar es Salaam   Hong Kong   Karachi
Kuala Lumpur   Madrid   Melbourne   Mexico City   Nairobi
New Delhi   Shanghai   Taipei   Toronto

With offices in

Argentina   Austria   Brazil   Chile   Czech Republic   France   Greece
Guatemala   Hungary   Italy   Japan   Poland   Portugal   Singapore
South Korea   Switzerland   Thailand   Turkey   Ukraine   Vietnam

Oxford is a registered trade mark of Oxford University Press
in the UK and in certain other countries

© Oxford University Press 2010

Authors: Chris Barcock, Liz Hanton, Mel Peeling, Alison Ross,
Christine Shaw Smith

The moral rights of the authors have been asserted

Database right Oxford University Press (maker)

First published 2010

British Library Cataloguing in Publication Data

Data available

ISBN 978-0-19-832946-6

10 9 8 7 6 5 4 3 2 1

Printed in Spain by Cayfosa-Impresia Ibérica

Paper used in the production of this book is a natural, recyclable product made
from wood grown in sustainable forests. The manufacturing process conforms to
the environmental regulations of the country of origin.

## Acknowledgements

The publisher and authors would like to thank the following for their permission
to reproduce photographs and other copyright material:
**p8**: relishtheglamour/Shutterstock; **p12t**: Miramax/Everett/Rex Features; **p12m**:
Moviworld/MK2/Miramax/The Kobal Collection; **p12-13**: Bettmann/Corbis; **p14t**:
Paul Yates/Fotolia; **p14-15**: Photodisc/OUP; **p15**: *Of Mice and Men* (1992) John
Malkovich, Gary Sinise MAM 051 Moviestore Collection ltd; **p16**: Mary Evans
Picture Library; **p17**: Everett Collection/Rex Features; **p18-19**: CaptureLight/
Shutterstock; **p19**: Radomir Rezny/Dreamstime, wessley/Shutterstock; **p20l**:
Imperial War Museum; **p20r**: Mary Evans Picture Library/Photolibrary; **p21**:
Paul Popper/Popperfoto/Getty Images; **p22**: Bildarchiv Preussischer Kulturbesitz;
**p23**: H. Armstrong Roberts/ClassicStock/Corbis; **p24ml**: Jason Stitt/Shutterstock;
**p24mr**: Monkey Business Images/Shutterstock; **p24bl**: R. Gino Santa Maria/
Shutterstock; **p24br**: Gelpi/Shutterstock; **p25**: Timo Kohlbacher/Shutterstock;
**p26**: Susannah Ireland/Rex Features; **p27t**: Janine Wiedel/Photographers Direct;
**p27b**: Ryan Rodrick Beiler/Shutterstock; **p28t**: Kieran Doherty/Reuters; **p28m**:
Kieran Doherty/Reuters; **p31**: Nathan Benn/Corbis; **p39m**: Eleanor Bentall/
Corbis; **p39b**: kristian sekulic/Shutterstock; **p40-41**: jarvis gray/Shutterstock;
**p40**: wessley/Shutterstock; **p43**: OUP; **p47**: Yuri Arcurs/Dreamstime; **p48t**: Galina
Barskaya/Big Stock Photo; **p48b**: Verity Johnson/Dreamstime; **p49**: Jeff Gynane/
Dreamstime; **P50**: Felipe Rodriguez/Alamy: **P53t**: Patrick Frilet/Rex Features;
**p53m**: Rune Hellestad/Corbis; P53m: Mary Evans Picture Library/Photolibrary;
**p53b**: WireImage/Getty; **p53l**: Bruce Shippee/Fotolia; **p54-55**: SkillUp/
Shutterstock; **p54t**: Nicole Gordine/Shutterstock, A.Karnaushenko/Shutterstock;
**p54m**: Alhovik/Shutterstock, Janaka Dharmasena/Shutterstock, **p54bl**:
Pertusinas/Shutterstock; **54br**: dyoma/Shutterstock; **P55m**: flavijus/Shutterstock;
**p55bl**: relishtheglamour/Shutterstock; **p55br**: buruhtan/Shutterstock; **p66**: clu/
iStockphoto; **p68**: Somos/OUP; **p69**: Stockbyte/Photolibrary; **p70**: Rune Johansen/
Photolibrary; **p71**: Simon Winnall/Photolibrary; **p79t**: Mark J. Terrill/AP Photo;
P79m: James D. Morgan/Rex Features; **p80**: Rexfeatures; **p81**: Toby Melville/
Reuters; **p82**: Comstock/OUP; **p83**: Tony Dejak/AP Photo; **p84t**: Rui Vieira/PA
Archive/Press Association Images; **p84m**: Adrian Sherratt/Rex Features; **p85**:
Ken McKay/Rex Features; **p86-87**: eAlisa/Shutterstock, Korionov/Shutterstock,
DrMadra/Shutterstock, Christos Georghiou/Shutterstock; **p88t**: Chris King/
OUP; **p88m**: Jeffrey Blackler/Alamy; P88b: Dean Mitchell/Shutterstock;
P89: Ross D. Franklin/AP Photo; **p90**: White/Photolibrary; **p93**: Steve Nagy/
Photolibrary; **p95**: Andre Maritz/Shutterstock; **p97m**: Emmanuel Faure/Stone/
Getty Images; **p97bl**: Masterfile; **p97br**: Objectif MC/Shutterstock; **p100**:
Global Warming Images/Alamy; **p105**: Monkey Business Images/Shutterstock;
**p116**: Oez/Shutterstock; **p118**: DW Photos/Shutterstock; **p119**: Roel Loopers/
Photolibrary; P120: Nick White and Fiona Jackson-Downes/Photolibrary;
**p121**: Christopher Hall/Fotolia; **p124m**: Joe Belanger/Shutterstock; **p124b**:
Fibobjects/Dreamstime, wessley/Shutterstock, Nataliya Peregudova/
Shutterstock; **p125t**: Image Wizard/Shutterstock; **p125m**: Ronald Grant
Archive; **p125b**: Ronald Grant Archive; **pp126-127**: BestPhoto1/Shutterstock;
**p126t**: Yuri Arcurs/Shutterstock; **p126bl**: Angela Hawkey/Shutterstock;
**p126br**: relishtheglamour/Shutterstock; **p127tl**: arenacreative/Shutterstock;
**p127tr** Dmitriy Shironosov/Shutterstock; **p127ml**: olly/Shutterstock; **p127mr**:
Roxana Gonzalez/Shutterstock; **p127b**: U.P.images_photo/Shutterstock;
**p130**: OUP, wessley/Shutterstock; **p131**: Godfer/Dreamstime; **p132t**: Brett
Mulcahy/Shutterstock; **p132m**: Surkov Vladimir/Shutterstock; **p132b**: Dennis
Macdonald/Photolibrary; **p134**: Stockbyte/OUP; **p138**: Luca Bruno Files/AP
Photo; **p139**: Sutton Images; **p144**: Pichugin Dmitry/Shutterstock, wessley/
Shutterstock; **p145**: Rybakov Vadim Grigor'evich/Shutterstock, wessley/
Shutterstock; **p151**: Shuedan/Shutterstock; **p153**: Bruce Martin/Alamyt;
**p153m**: relishtheglamour/Shutterstock; **p154**: Lluís Real/Photolibrary; **p156**:
Monkey Business Images/Shutterstock; **p159**: Tom Hevezi/AP Photo; **p160**:
Derwent Valley Mills Partnership, wessley/Shutterstock; **p162**: wessley/
Shutterstock; **p163**: Le Do/Shutterstock; **p165l**: Picture Perfect/Rex Features;
**p165r**: Cynoclub/Shutterstock.

Illustrations by Ben Swift, Flora Douville, Oxford Designers & Illustrators
Rheannon Cummins, Theresa Tibbetts, Tom Genower.  Cover illustration: Sian
Thomas

The publisher and authors are grateful for permission to reprint the following
copyright material:
**Simon Armitage**: 'Poem' from *Zoom!* (Bloodaxe, 2002), copyright © Simon
Armitage 1989, reprinted by permission of Bloodaxe Books, and 'About His
Person' from *Kid* (Faber, 1992), copyright © Simon Armitage 1992, reprinted
by permission of Faber & Faber Ltd.; **Simon Barnes**: extract from 'The worst
act of cheating in the history of sport', *The Times*, 17.9.2009, copyright © *The
Times* 2009, reprinted by permission of News International Syndication.; **Bill
Bryson**: extracts from *Notes from a Small Island* (Black Swan, 1996), reprinted by
permission of The Random House Group Ltd.; **Sir Winston Churchill**: extract
from 'Fight them on the beaches' speech, 4 June 1940, reprinted by permission
of Curtis Brown Ltd, London on behalf of The Estate of Winston Churchill.;
**John Cleese** with **Connie Booth**: extract from 'A Touch of Class' from *The
Complete Fawlty Towers* (Methuen, 1988), reprinted by permission of David
Wilkinson Associates.; **Carol-Ann Duffy**: 'Stealing' from *Selling Manhattan*
(Anvil, 1987), reprinted by permission of Anvil Press Poetry.; **Stephen Fry**:
extract from *Stephen Fry in America* (HarperCollins, 2008), copyright © Stephen
Fry 2008, reprinted by permission of HarperCollins Publishers Ltd.; **Athol
Fugard**: extracts from *Tsotsi* (Canongate, 2009), originally published by Ad
Donker, South Africa 1980, reprinted by permission of Canongate Books and
William Morris Endeavour Entertainment for the author.; **Nikki Garnett**:
extract on Morecambe from www.citycoastcountryside.co.uk, reprinted by
permission of the author and Apparatus Marketing.; **Edward Gorman**:
extract from 'F1 boss ousted over driver ordered to crash', *The Times*, 17.9.2009,
copyright © *The Times* 2009, reprinted by permission of News International
Syndication.; **Mark Haddon**: opening extract from *The Curious Incident of
the Dog in the Night-Time* (David Fickling/Jonathan Cape, 2003), reprinted by
permission of The Random House Group Ltd.; **Annabel Kenzie**: extracts
from 'The Beautiful Game' in *Smart English: Progress in Afs (Smart Learning)*,
reprinted by permission of the author.; **Safari India**: extract from 'A typical
day on Safari in India' from http://www.safariindia.co.uk, reprinted by
permission of Safari India LLP.; **John Steinbeck**: extracts from *Of Mice and
Men* (Penguin, 2006), copyright © John Steinbeck 1937, 1965, reprinted by
permission of Penguin Books Ltd.; **Jonathan Tulloch**: extracts from *The Season
Ticket* (Jonathan Cape, 2000), reprinted by permission of The Random House
Group Ltd.; **Wildlife Tours in India**: extract from http://www.wildlife-tour-
india.com, copyright © Wildlife Tours.http://www.wildlife-tour-india.com,/;
**John Wyndham**: opening extract from *The Chrysalids* (Michael Joseph 1955,
Penguin Books 1958, 1979, 2000), reprinted by permission of David Higham
Associates.; **Benjamin Zephaniah**: 'Three Black Males' and lines from 'Chant
of a Homesick Nigga' from *Too Black, Too Strong* (Bloodaxe, 2003), reprinted by
permission of Bloodaxe Books.

Although we have made every effort to trace and contact all copyright holders
before publication this has not been possible in all cases. If notified, the
publisher will rectify any errors or omissions at the earliest opportunity.